Three Proposals

A Canyon Road Christmas Love Story

Book 4

Thea Thomas

Books by Thea Thomas

The Canyon Road Love Stories series:
Canyon Road
One Love
Two Weddings
Three Proposals

YA:
The City Under Seattle Series:
The People in the Mirror
Meechie in the Mirror

Dark Urban:
Amethyst Dreams
Porcelain Claws

Three Proposals

A Canyon Road Christmas Love Story

Book 4

Thea Thomas

Three Proposals
Book 4:
A Canyon Road Christmas Love Story
Contemporary Sweet Romance
Thea Thomas

Emerson & Tilman, Publishers
129 Pendleton Way #55
Washougal, WA 98671

All Rights Reserved
No part of this publication may be reproduced, distributed, or transmitted in any form, or by any means, including photocopying, recording, or other electronic or mechanical methods, without the prior written permission of the author, except brief quotations in critical reviews and other noncommercial uses permitted by copyright law.
This is a work of fiction.
Names, characters, places, and incidents are fictional.

Book & cover design by Emerson & Tilman
Thea@EmersonandTilman.com

Three Proposals
Copyright © Thea Thomas/Emerson & Tilman

Paperback ISBN: 978-1-947151-72-7

[1. FICTION/Romance/Contemporary
2. FICTION/Contemporary Women
3. FICTION/Romance/General] I. Title
BIC: FM
First Edition

DEDICATION:

*To All Who Believe
That the Meaning of Christmas
Is Love*

Chapter 1

Three Proposals is *Book 4* in the *Canyon Road Love Stories* series, a sweet, contemporary romance novella with an old-fashioned Christmas theme. Here's a thumbnail sketch of characters if you've not read the three previous books:

SAGE and MICHAEL meet in *Canyon Road*. Michael's UNCLE ANTHONY lives in the mansion next to Sage's AUNT VICTORIA's mansion. Sage came to live with her aunt after her anthropologist parents—her mother a Zuni Indian—were killed in a small plane crash. When the story opens, Sage's Aunt Victoria has died but a few days before in a horseback riding accident.

Michael "rescues" Sage on his way to visit his uncle, when her car dies in the middle of the road at the bottom of her driveway. After he gets her car started and out of the road, he goes on his way. They are each privately smitten by the other, but assume their paths will never cross again.

However! Fate will have its way, and they encounter one another again and again—with mounting confusion over who's who, they each believe the other is in a relationship.

TINA is Sage's best friend, involved in an abusive relationship with Aunt Victoria's evil attorney, BILL RATTNOR. (Not all attorneys are evil. But this one is!) He has a dreadful confrontation—not with Tina, but with Sage—that at least ends Tina's involvement with him. The good news is, Tina subsequently meets JOHN. *Finally! A good guy!*

MILLICENT—Millie in Book 1, but Millicent afterward—is Michael's best friend. She sees him through his depression, while her unrequited love for him goes entirely unnoticed.

EATON and CLARA are the ever-present staff, overlooking the well-being of their charges.

Book 2, One Love, is primarily Michael's AUNT ALISON's story. After the heartbreak of the dissolution of her marriage, she moves from Southern California to San Francisco and becomes serious about her art. She begins to teach art classes, and, much to her surprise, her art becomes hugely popular, and she establishes a name for herself in the San Francisco art scene.

Alison is beautiful, sweet, kind, and somewhat famous. Not surprisingly, she has several suitors. Who will capture her heart?

Book 3, Two Weddings, Millicent blossoms. She has proven to have a magnificent head for business, and Sage—who has *no* head for business at all, and doesn't care to—hires Millicent to handle the extensive financial concerns Aunt Victoria has left her with.

Who gets married in *Two Weddings*? You'll need to read the book!

EMDEE is a darling little black dog who literally comes flying into Millicent's life. She always answers a question directed at her with a bark.

Don't you Emdee?

"Woof!"

ERIC is Michael's childhood best pal. Gorgeous? Oh, yes! *Read on* ....

Chapter 1

December 22
Anthony & Alison

"Oh! Watch out, Eaton, that box above is about to topple on you!" Alison stepped back to avoid it toppling on her as well, as Eaton exhumed boxes and red and green totes of Christmas decorations, buried in the dark recesses of the attic.

"I've got it," Eaton exclaimed, abandoning the box he'd been reaching for and capturing the offender. He stepped down from the ladder and put it on the growing pile of boxes and plastic totes, then climbed back on the ladder.

Alison surveyed the pile, now taller than herself. "Goodness! I forgot how many Christmas tchotchkes and boxes of bunting and trimmings we have!"

"With several boxes yet to go," Eaton turned to look down at her. At that moment, a brightly-colored Christmas jester, appearing from seemingly nowhere, fell on Eaton's head, draping its colorful limbs over his face.

Alison burst into laughter. "Oh no, Eaton, the little jester has captured you!" She reached up and plucked it from his face.

"So it would seem," Eaton agreed with quiet reserve.

"What's all the levity?" Anthony called, coming up the narrow attic stairs. "You're having too much fun—digging out the Christmas decorations is supposed to be serious business!" He came up to Alison, brushed some dust off her cheek, and kissed her.

"Oh, darling, you just missed seeing this little jester come out of nowhere and land right on Eaton's head!"

Anthony took the jester from Alison and looked at him sternly. "We'll have none of that! You have a job to do, and it's not to make Eaton look foolish."

"Well, sir, in point of fact," Eaton came down from the ladder with yet another box, "that is rather precisely the business of jesters. To play the fool, and to show people the fool in themselves."

"*Ah!* In which case," Anthony addressed the jester, "carry on, good fellow, jest away." He handed the doll back to Alison. "I came up here, my love, to see if I could help with this enormous project."

"*Fantastic!* If you'd haul some of these boxes and totes downstairs, that would be a huge help. Each one has written on it where it goes."

"Useful at last," Anthony quipped. "I'm on it!" He picked up the two top boxes and headed downstairs. "Don't you lift a thing, my pet, Eaton and I will handle it." He reached the bottom of the stairs. "Won't we?"

"Indeed, sir," Eaton replied, coming down from the ladder with the next box.

Alison took it from him. "Don't overdo it, Eaton."

"Of course not." He gave Alison a studied glance, then looked away.

"What, Eaton?"

"Nothing." He paused. "Well, not nothing. I'm just so … it's wonderful having you back in the house. It gives me great pleasure to be poking around in the attic looking for Christmas decorations, after those years of … *not* poking around in the attic looking for Christmas decorations."

"Oh, Eaton, you're going to make me cry."

"Surely not my intent, Miss Alison."

"You know what I mean."

"I do." He climbed back up the ladder. "I believe there are only two more boxes here, stuck back in the corner. And then the real work begins!"

"Fun, every minute."

"Agreed."

Anthony came back up the stairs. "Boxes properly delivered, and more on their way." He picked up the next two boxes on the pile.

"Wonderful," Alison said, just as Anthony's phone rang.

He set the boxes down and looked at his phone. His brow furrowed. "*Hmmm*, I'd better take this," he went down the stairs. Alison heard a note of surprise in his voice after he answered the phone, followed by a quiet and serious-sounding conversation. She heard something in his tone she didn't recognize. She waited for him to return and tell her what was going on.

But he didn't come back up the narrow stairs into the attic.

"*Strange*," she said softly.

"Somewhat," Eaton agreed, coming down from the ladder with the last two boxes. "As I have these in hand, I believe I'll carry them on down to their destinations."

Alison nodded absentmindedly. She stood there, waiting for Anthony to return, but he did not. Very odd, indeed. Frowning, she picked up one of the totes and headed down the stairs, taking it to its respective room. After she'd set the box down, she looked around for Anthony, but couldn't find him.

She went up into the attic, hoping he'd gone back up when she was in the bedroom, but he wasn't there, either. Eaton, loaded up with three boxes, was headed down the stairs.

"Have you seen Anthony?"

"No, I haven't. It appears the call was quite important."

Alison nodded. "Even so, the Christmas decorations must be put up!" she said with false cheer, picking up two boxes and following Eaton down the stairs.

* *

When all the boxes had been set in their various rooms, making the mansion appear depressingly cluttered, Alison literally and figuratively rolled up her sleeves, and with Eaton and Clara, began opening the boxes and totes to sort out what went where.

"I made mulled wine," Clara said as she and Alison hung red and green bunting around one of the bedrooms.

"Lovely, Clara. Though more a treat for later, after we're finished running up and down ladders."

"It's non-alcoholic."

"Oh-ho, then, bring it on!" Alison stepped down from the ladder and looked at their handiwork. "Pretty, yes?"

"Beautiful, Alison. It's wonderful to have the Christmas decorations out of the musty old boxes. Well, we've completed three rooms, time for a break!"

Alison laughed. "At that rate, we'll never get done, but yes, absolutely time for a break."

They wandered down the hall heading for the stairs when Alison heard Eaton and Anthony chatting in one of the bedrooms.

"There's Anthony! He disappeared on Eaton and me, just when he'd committed to help us take the boxes and totes down from the attic, and I haven't seen him since!" She stepped into the room where the two men were talking. Their conversation broke off.

"Am I interrupting?" She looked from one to the other.

"Of course not, Miss Alison," Eaton said. "We were discussing the heady subject of the height at which the bunting ought to be placed."

"Important decision!" Alison moved over to Anthony and put her arm around his waist. "What's the consensus, as I see only a half-opened box with bunting hanging out." Anthony stiffened ever so slightly at her touch. Shocked, she took a step away from him.

"I believe," Eaton continued, "it ought to be hung just above the door, while Anthony suggested it go near the ceiling."

"Did you?" She looked at Anthony, but he refused to return her glance.

"Well, I did. But I see now, I was wrong. Carry on, Eaton. As always, you know best." He exited the room, but not without having to negotiate around Clara, who stood in the doorway.

Alison looked from Eaton to Clara. *"What was that?"*

"Goodness," Clara said softly. "Something taking his mind, that's for sure."

Alison returned her glance to Eaton, perched on the ladder, empty-handed, having been waiting for Anthony to hand him the bunting. He said nothing, but gave a little nod.

"Well," Alison reached into the box and handed Eaton the sparkly gold and red decoration, "we won't let it disrupt our mood! He'll sort it out."

"Yes," Clara agreed. "He always does." She helped Alison unfurl the bunting.

"Eaton, Clara has mulled wine waiting for us, so let's finish this room and take a well-earned break!"

"Mulled wine!?"

"Non-alcoholic," Clara added.

"Even so, this project will never get done before Sage and Michael arrive if we take breaks every couple of rooms."

"You know we'll get it done," Clara affirmed. "And what's more, Sage and Michael won't care if we *don't* get it done! Besides, they're staying at Sage's. We don't even know yet for sure if any of their entourage will be staying here."

"All true," Alison agreed, so completely engaged in her concern regarding Anthony's peculiar, unpleasant, behavior that she lost her Christmas mood.

Still! Sage and Michael were coming, and that, for the moment, was what she looked forward to with happy anticipation.

Millicent & Eric

"What a disappointment," Millicent said, looking at the three small boxes on the floor before her. "I ransacked the attic for Christmas decorations, but this is all I could come up with."

"It'll be fine, Millicent," Eric said, stooping over to open one of the boxes. "*Hmmm,*" he added, as he looked at the sad, wilted, contents.

"*Oh! Awful!* It gets worse." She opened the next box. Several moths flew out, along with a musty smell. "*And yet worse.* What am I to do? Sage and Michael will be here in a couple days—their first time in the mansion since they got married. I don't even know when they're coming, exactly, since they're driving and 'taking their time.'"

"I'm sure they'll call and let you know when they'll arrive."

"No calls. Aunt Pelipa said it's to be an 'old-fashioned Christmas.' I wouldn't be surprised if they came on horse-drawn sleds."

"Unlikely, sweetheart, from New Mexico to California, even if it *is* Christmas."

"You know what I mean."

Eric took Millicent by the hand, and led her to the attic steps, then pulled her down to sit cozily on his lap. "If Sage doesn't have Christmas decorations, it'll be fine. We'll all be together, and isn't that all that matters?" He hugged her close.

"No. It matters *the most*, but it's not *all* that matters. Sage doesn't know the condition of these sad, ancient, ruined, Christmas decorations. She probably has in mind lovely, sparkly red and green and silver and gold festooning the mansion for her first Christmas married to Michael, and with all their family and friends here.

"However," she gestured to the forlorn, dusty boxes, "it will be barren of red and green and silver and gold sparkly." Vexed, Millicent stood up.

"Yet more weird will be the snow machine I ordered, which is coming tomorrow." Millicent sighed. "I had such a romantic picture of a lovely, soft snowfall, even if fake, outside the windows around the fireplace. But it'll just seem weird without any decorations. I haven't even gotten a tree, which I hope to do tomorrow. I want to get a real tree, especially given that the snow will be fake. But again, a tree without ornaments."

She hurried to the last unopened box. "Maybe there's at least some ornaments for a tree." She pulled out a box, looked at its contents and sighed, holding it up for Eric to see. It contained ornaments, true. Every one of them broken.

"Why would someone pack away broken ornaments?"

"I imagine that the box was dropped, or something heavy fell on it. It's a bit dented on this side."

"So. No ornaments. No point in getting a tree. No decent decorations. It will not be the perfect Christmas." Millicent turned her back on the miserable Christmas decorations. "I am *not* happy."

"Doesn't Sage have a 'miscellaneous funds' account? I know you've mentioned it."

"Yes. But …."

"But what? This is an important moment for the use of miscellaneous funds. So close to Christmas the selection of decorations might be pretty slim, but I bet we can come up with enough to make the place festive."

Millicent shook her head, despondent. "I don't feel very hopeful, but at this point, what choice do I have?"

"You're so adorable when you let me have my way," Eric stood and led her away from the wretched boxes and down the stairs.

"Don't get used to it!" Millicent advised. "But your plan is better than mine—which is nothing, other than to stand around in despair."

* *

They returned five hours later, laden with three trips of bags and boxes from Eric's truck into the mansion.

"Thank goodness for your truck," Millicent chirped. "I can't believe we got all these beautiful decorations at the last minute and, it seems to me, for very little money."

"Have you never bought Christmas decorations?"

"No. I haven't. When I was mother to my little siblings, I had no money for such luxury. Then, when they grew up and I lived alone, why bother? In point of fact, I'm not sure how to put all these decorations up so they look right."

"Not to worry, love-of-mine. I am the Christmas Magician, and I'm here to make magic!"

Millicent threw her arms around his neck and kissed him. "Wonderful, Christmas Magician. Please, make magic!"

* *

By early evening they'd made a notable dent in the pile of sparkly red and green and silver and gold, while the rooms took on a reflective glow.

"Let's take a break," Millicent said, plopping down on the sofa before the fireplace.

"Excellent! I'll start a fire, so you can get the full effect of our efforts."

Millicent allowed herself the pleasure of watching Eric's deft moves as he placed twigs and wood strategically in the fireplace, then lit it. His muscular forearms glowed in the firelight as it grew. Altogether yummy to watch, she told herself.

Finally, he came over and sat by her.

"You're … so beautiful," she whispered as he put his arm around her. She curled up in his embrace, contented as any little kitten, and her little black dog, Emdee, scurried up from wherever she'd been sleeping to join them.

"Where have you been, little girl?" Millicent asked, putting the dog on her lap. "There now, the three of us, little bugs in a rug, cozy and warm." She studied the shiny silver and gold bunting around the fireplace, and the little stand-alone Christmas pretties they'd gotten and placed on the end tables and mantle. *"Nice, nice, nice!* We'll get a tree tomorrow and put it there, by that window. The fake snow will come softly down. Will it not be lovely?"

"It *is* lovely, Millicent," Eric said, petting Emdee. "Almost perfect."

"Almost perfect? I think, *perfect!"*

There was a long pause. Millicent saw the fire crackling, heard the grandfather clock ticking, felt Emdee breathing in her lap. And sensed that something … *something unanticipated* was about to happen.

Eric removed his arm from around her and stood. "I wanted to do this on Christmas Eve, or even on Christmas Eve Eve, but since we don't know when the house will be full of people, and since right now, we're in a glow of Christmas garlands and pretty things …." He pulled a tiny box from his pocket and got down on bended knee before her. Opening the box, he revealed something that caught the firelight, out-sparkling all the sparkle they'd put up.

"My darling Millicent, I love you with all my heart, and I simply cannot imagine life without you. Nor do I care to. I only have one simple question, which is, will you marry me?"

Millicent jumped up, sending Emdee to the sofa.

"Oh, Eric! Why? Why are you asking this question?" Millicent felt shock and distress.

"Not entirely the response I was expecting," Eric said, closing the little box and putting it back in his pocket.

"I can't … no! Why would you change the way things are? It's working perfectly. In all my life, whenever there's been a big change, it has been a disaster."

"It won't be a disaster. Do you not love me?"

"I love you, Eric. I love you with all my heart. You know that. And that's why I say no. *No!*" She strode back and forth in front of the fireplace. "Why would you do this now, when I have so much to do and so much to think about? *Why?*"

Eric sat on the sofa and patted Emdee, who whimpered quietly. "I—apparently foolishly—thought you would say yes. And I thought everyone who loves us would be so happy for us, when we are all together during Christmas. I had a picture I thought you'd share."

"Oh, goodness!" Millicent cried. "You're so much more romantic than I am. My only picture for the next few days is to get through them, with everyone having had a charming Christmas. No thought at all about myself. Not even a mental image of me in the picture. I do believe, Eric, that you love me more than I do. Yet more reason for me to say no!"

"Can you really say you've never thought of us being married?"

"Ahh …." Millicent paused in her pacing for a moment. "I, ah, I don't know. I mean, I can't think of it now. Such thoughts have not been good for me in the past."

"Oh!" Eric said, insight striking. "Because of Michael."

"Just … please, Eric, don't say it. Don't go there."

"Is it possible … that you're still in love with Michael?"

"No, Eric, I am not. No. But well, yes, when I had thoughts of that nature, they were wrong."

"Not wrong, Millicent. Just … misdirected. But with me, they're not misdirected."

Emdee whimpered and looked piteously at Millicent.

"I feel terrible making my little dog cry."

"What about me?"

"You're not crying."

"Not exactly. But I'm in shock."

"Please, Eric, don't be." Millicent wanted to rush to both of them, but she couldn't move. She couldn't think. *She. Could. Not. Think.* "I …" she looked around dazed, "Eric, I have so much I have to do. I mean, I *must* do. And right now, I can't even *think*."

Eric stood, came over to her and walked her back to the sofa and Emdee. "Just sit here, Millicent."

She sat.

"We'll table this discussion. I understand that you have so much to do. That you only have so much bandwidth to accomplish all you must accomplish, and that I've thrown a pretty large rock in the pond of your thoughts."

"A boulder. Yes."

"A boulder. We'll just rewind this evening back to before I stood up. You here." He picked up the little black dog and placed her on Millicent's lap. "Your little dog here." He then sat beside her and put his arm around her. "And me here, beside you, the three of us cozy 'little bugs in a rug,' enjoying the fire."

Emdee snuggled down, yawned, and put her nose in the crook of Millicent's elbow.

"Better?" Eric asked.

"Better. But one cannot un-experience an experience."

"Agreed. But one—or two—can save it for some other moment to re-contemplate. I'm surprised. I'm disappointed. But I love you. I'm not going to love someone else. And if not being married to me is part of who you are, then I must love that part, as well."

Millicent let herself relax just a tiny bit into Eric's embrace, though feeling so completely out of sorts. "You are a strange and beautiful man."

"And you are a strange and beautiful woman, my love."

Michael's Decorations

Although they sat before the fire in what appeared to be companionable silence, Millicent's thoughts were in turmoil. Eric had just asked her to marry him. She tried to replay the moment when he opened the little box, and the light sparkled off the beautiful ring.

Goodness! She had no idea what the ring looked like! She'd just gone into shock. She remembered jumping up and moving away. Moving away from this amazing moment, away from this amazing man. But she still could not say "yes."

Fear. Plain and simple. Fear reigned in that moment.

Her phone rang, and, although she loathed to talk to anyone, longing to simply sort out her feelings, she glanced at her phone.

"It's Alison," she said, answering the call.

"Merry Christmas, Alison."

"Merry Christmas, dear. I know you're crazy busy pulling the place together for the pending company, but Eaton and I have been going through boxes and totes of

Christmas decorations, and there are a few here that were Michael's favorites when he was a child, as his family always spent Christmas with us. It dawned on me that these decorations should be there, in his environment when he and Sage come. What do you think?"

Millicent jumped up in excitement. "Oh, Alison, what a fantastic idea. I'm so glad you thought of it. There were no usable decorations in the attic, so Eric and I went out and bought a slew of generic baubles and swags—they're better than nothing. But Michael will be so touched to see his own childhood memories here! Do you want us to come over and get them?"

"No. Actually, Eaton is loading them up as we speak. We'll be there shortly, if that's okay with you."

"More than okay. See you soon!" She turned to Eric, her face glowing. "I guess you got the gist of that. They're bringing over Michael's own favorite childhood decorations."

Eric gave her a big hug. "Wonderful! I think the moment calls for gingerbread. I've been going to bake some for the last couple days, and now's the time!"

"That's a great idea—I'll be your assistant until they arrive."

They went into the kitchen, Emdee running circles around them, barking and leaping about with unreserved doggie glee.

As Eric gathered the ingredients and preheated the oven, Millicent got out bowls and pans and utensils.

"Is that good?" She gestured to the array of cookware on the counter.

Eric laughed. "Good and more than good. I think I'll make enough gingerbread for, say, around a dozen people, not an army!"

Millicent surveyed the array she'd set out. "Oh, I guess I did overdo it a bit," she giggled, returning a few of the pots and pans to their homes.

Quick as a wink, Eric had the gingerbread mixed up and batter poured into two square pans and popped into the oven.

"*Lovely!*" Millicent exclaimed, her wonder never ceasing at Eric's amazing skill in the kitchen. "Not only will we have gingerbread for a treat after putting up the decorations Alison is bringing, but the house will soon smell so lovely and Christmas-y."

The front door chimes rang and Millicent and Eric scurried to open the door. Alison and Eaton stepped into the foyer, each carrying a big box.

"Let's take these boxes to the dining room table so we can sort through them and decide what goes where," Alison suggested.

"Sure!" Millicent agreed.

"What smells so fantastic?" Alison inhaled deeply.

"Eric whipped up some gingerbread and popped it in the oven. A treat for us later!"

"Wonderful! And guess what? Eaton and I brought some mulled wine that Clara made today. It started out non-alcoholic while we were working at putting up the decorations. But I believe Clara added a bit of real wine to it before putting it in the giant thermos."

"Bring it in," Eric said. "I'll put it on the stove to warm up, and add to the festive aroma."

"Happily!" Eaton put down the box he carried and went back out to the car. When he returned, he and Eric put the mulled wine on the stove while Alison and Millicent opened the boxes.

"Where's Anthony?" Millicent asked as she carefully poked through the paper-wrapped items in the box.

A small frown crossed Alison's features. "I don't exactly know. He was in great spirits this morning, and then he got a phone call, and has been taciturn and unavailable all day."

Millicent paused, a half-unwrapped decoration in hand. "That's … strange."

"Very strange."

"What do you think …."

At that moment, Eric and Eaton joined them. "Mulled wine and gingerbread soon available to those who have earned their Christmas cheer," Eric said, jovially. "And that's everyone in this room!"

Emdee barked, tail wagging.

"Yes, even you. We have for you your own special treats." Eric reached down and patted her. "Eaton tells me that you've brought over some large outdoor decorations, so we'll get at putting those up and lighted, while you attend to these little delicate items."

"Sounds perfect," Millicent nodded.

"Is there anything we should carry upstairs up for you first?"

"No, I think we can handle it."

"All righty then, off we go."

"What about the gingerbread? Won't it be ready to come out of the oven soon?"

"Don't worry about it, I've got it covered!" Eric answered.

"A man of many talents," Alison quipped.

Eric grinned like a little boy as he and Eaton left the dining room, happy with the projects at hand.

"This box is completely Michael's things," Alison said, "and this one is just an excess of other Christmas ornaments."

"Are they tree ornaments?"

"They can be."

"Excellent. Like I said, Eric and I ran out and bought everything you see here," she made a sweeping gesture about the room, Christmas candles stood on the mantle and table, a silver and gold sparkly swag adorned the mantle, and a red and green "Merry Christmas" hung across the living room. "But the options for tree ornaments were very few at the last minute. Shall we take the 'Michael box' upstairs to their room?"

"That's a good idea," Alison agreed.

They went upstairs and down the hall to the room that had been Sage's during her childhood.

"Oh! Are they not staying in the master suite?" Alison asked.

"No. Sage was very firm about not wanting to stay in the master suite, as it had, of course, been her Aunt's 'domain.' She said she didn't want any 'ghosts of Christmas Past' rattling its chains around them during her first Christmas with Michael."

Alison chuckled, but it wasn't funny. It was sad that Sage's aunt had left such a gloomy legacy.

They stepped into Sage's sweet room, pastel and cheerful. "Awfully girly, but I don't think Michael will mind," Millicent said.

"It's so charming and *sooo* Sage." Alison put the box she carried on the bed and sat down beside it. Millicent sat on the other side of the box, and they began pulling out the various little items … several bears in assorted red and green sweaters, hats, and scarves.

"Oh," Millicent giggled, "I never knew he liked bears! These are adorable …."

"Yes, he had quite the thing for bears. Every Christmas he'd look for his bear, not happy until he unwrapped it. Anthony started the tradition with this one." Alison held up a tiny bear, no more than two inches tall, dressed in a red jacket and green pants, topped with a tiny red hat, and a jingling bell on its pointed tip.

"It looks like an antique and rather Eastern European," Millicent observed.

"Good eye, Millicent. Exactly right. It belonged to Anthony's grandfather who came to the states many, many years ago." Alison stood up and looked about the room. "I guess I'll put them on this chest of drawers across from the bed, where he can easily enjoy them." She moved a few things about on the dresser and then lined the bears up in a particular order. She stepped back and admired her project. "Nice. They're in the order we gave them to him."

"How do you remember that?" Millicent asked.

"I don't know! I just do. Now then, let's check out the other things in the box."

Several other trinkets and ornaments were placed about the room until they came to the bottom of the box. Millicent watched as Alison carefully pulled out the large item, apparently rather heavy, wrapped in layers of fabric and paper, which Alison pulled away slowly, almost ritualistically.

"The suspense is enticing," Millicent whispered.

Alison nodded, saying nothing. Finally, she revealed a large snow globe containing a beautiful, delicate, nativity scene. "This was his very favorite ornament of all. He would sit for an hour watching the snow fall around the scene."

Alison's voice became soft. "One Christmas Eve he was engrossed in his ... meditation is all I can call it ... of this scene. Company was soon coming and the house would be full of people. I'd wanted him to do a couple things for me—I don't remember what now, but when I sat beside him he said, 'Aunt Alison, this is very important. Do you know what I know, looking at this?' 'No, dear,' I said, 'what do you know?' 'I know that this baby represents love. And that this round globe is like the earth, and the snow is like love and the baby is bringing love to earth.'" Alison's voice caught.

Tears came to Millicent's eyes, imaging the little boy Michael having this pure and innocent insight into the meaning of Christmas. *"That's ... so ... touching,"* Millicent whispered.

Alison nodded and placed the globe on the bedside table. "I'm sure he'll be happy to see it after all these years. I'm really glad Eaton was able to find this box. It didn't get pulled out this morning when he pulled out nearly twenty red and green totes and Christmas marked boxes. This afternoon I was thinking about that moment Michael and I shared and realized that I didn't see his box. I asked Easton to see if he could find it, and happily, he was able to 'unearth' it among that muddle of stuff in the attic."

A burst of guffaws from outside interrupted their moment. Millicent and Alison went to the window to see what was so amusing. Eric and Eaton were struggling with a giant candy cane, attempting to lean it over the sidewalk in front of the door, but, instead, the hook of the cane was wrapped around Eric's neck. Not the intention!

"That candy cane appears to have it in for Eric. Not often one hears Eaton actually laugh out loud," Millicent said.

"True! A delightful sound! I've been so looking forward to this Christmas, the first for Sage and Michael …." Alison trailed off.

"I'm sure whatever is taking Anthony's mind will get sorted out. Or he'll share it with you."

Alison raised her eyebrows. "Very attentive of you, Millicent, dear. Thank you. I'm sure it will all sort out. But there was only one other Christmas when he behaved like this …."

"No, Alison. This Christmas is not like that Christmas. He dotes on you. He's not about to let anything disrupt your relationship."

"I certainly hope not. But, allow me to change the subject—how are things between you and Eric? They seem wonderful."

"Oh, goodness! You *would* ask!" Millicent fell into silence, unable to say anything further.

"Did I step into something?"

"Let's just say that I learned earlier this evening that Eric's picture of where we are is different from mine."

"Oh?"

"He's … much more romantic, I think, than I am."

The front door opened and Eric called up the stairs. "We need some additional input about where to place things … can you join us?"

"Sure," Millicent answered. "We'll be right down."

She and Alison exchanged a glance, suspending the current conversation. They gathered the papers and fabrics that wrapped the ornaments and stuck them back in the box, then stood in the doorway taking in the effect for a few moments.

"*Precious!*" Alison whispered.

Millicent nodded agreement.

Chapter 4

Tree Talk

Alison and Millicent stepped out the front door into the nearly balmy southern California December evening. The two seven-foot tall candy canes now appeared to be behaving properly, leaning companionably against one another, their red and white striped lights rotating up and down.

"Perfect," Alison patted Eric on the back. "I'm glad to see you escaped with your neck intact."

"Yes," Millicent agreed. "We peeked out the window when it sounded like you boys were having too much fun, only to see one of these canes closing in on your jugular."

Eric chuckled. "It was a battle for a few moments, but I won, and let the canes know who's boss around here."

"That would be me," Eaton interjected somberly.

"He's right. He made the giant candy canes behave." Eric waved at a couple of large items that Millicent couldn't quite make out in the gathering evening shadows. "We have to figure where to put these amazing horses, so we've recruited the two of you, with your impeccable sense of balance and beauty, to direct us."

"Flattery will get you everywhere." Alison moved to a spot in the front yard a bit away from the candy canes, but still in the glow of their light. "When we had the candy canes in our yard, we put each of the horses about this distance on either side of the candy canes. They have their own light, but it's much subtler."

"Looks good!" Eric picked up one of the still paper-covered figures, a couple of feet taller than himself, and placed it where Alison stood, while Eaton carried the other across the yard in line with the first.

"Horses? Shades of *The Nutcracker*." Millicent exclaied. She started removing the foamy wrapping from the figure nearest her and Eaton joined in, while Eric and Alison did the same with the other figure. Finally, they revealed two beautiful horses, one with a little boy and the other with a little girl on its back, both horses rearing up, fully standing on their hind legs, the pretty children smiling happily.

"Now for their lights," Eaton said. He thrashed around in the subdued light of the candy canes and the front door lighting and soon had the light cords in hand. "For the full effect, you'll want to turn off the yard lights."

Millicent scurried inside to turn off the lights and then returned outside.

"Okay," Easton said, "here goes. Let's hope they work, they haven't been out of storage for nearly a decade." He plugged the two plugs together, and a beautiful glow emanated from both horses and children.

"*Ohhhh!*" Everyone sighed.

"*It's too beautiful,*" Millicent whispered.

Eric put his arm around her. "It's going to be ... the perfect Christmas."

"Let's drink to that," Alison said. "And have some gingerbread!"

"Yes, let's," Eric agreed.

They all took another moment to contemplate the lovely lighted decorations, and then headed for the kitchen.

"I came in and put the gingerbread on cooling racks, right before the candy cane attacked me. It looks perfect."

"And smells absolutely wonderful," Alison exclaimed. "I wish Anthony was here. I'm sure he'd love this."

"Oh! Why isn't he?" Eric asked, placing the gingerbread on a Christmas platter, while Millicent got out some colorful plates and mugs.

"I don't know. He seems to be stricken with an Ebenezer Scrooge flu bug, or some such."

Eaton chuckled softly. "Good one, Miss Alison. But I'm sure he'll come into Christmas Present before the ghost of Christmas Past rattles its chains."

"Oh dear!" Millicent stopped setting out plates in mid-motion. "Another invocation of Christmas Past ghosts. I'll have no dreary, chain rattling ghosts in this house!"

Eric ladled the mulled wine into the mugs. "I second that incantation. No dreary, chain-rattling, Christmas Past ghosts in Sage's mansion!"

"*Hear! Hear!*" they all cheered.

"To a perfect first Christmas for Sage and Michael!" Millicent declared.

"*Hear! Hear!*" they cheered with yet more enthusiasm. "To a perfect first Christmas!"

* *

"**I** know you probably have so much more decorating and the like to attend to at your own place, but might it be possible for you to help us figure out what we're doing with the rest of this froufrou?" Millicent pled after their festive gingerbread and mulled wine break.

"I'd love to," Alison said, cutting off another little sliver of gingerbread. "Just need a bit more! But we're encroaching upon Eaton's private time."

"I'm quite enjoying myself," Eaton said.

"Let us continue, then!" Alison stood and stretched. "The fireplace looks lovely, Millicent."

"Thank you. I mean, Eric thanks you. I just helped him. We're getting a tree tomorrow, and thank goodness, I'm much relieved to know that Eric will have an eye for making it look gorgeous."

"How big of a tree do you plan on getting?"

"I have no idea! How big should the tree be, Eric?"

"Well, I'd say a good eight to ten feet to properly compliment the space."

"*Ten feet tall!*" Millicent exclaimed. "Goodness! Once again, gratitude that I'm not left alone with Christmas details. Give me a spreadsheet, I'll make short work of it. Put me in charge of decorating for the holidays, I'm at sea."

Alison laughed. "You won't drown with Eric's help. I agree with you, Eric. A nice nine or ten-foot tree will be beautiful with these twelve-foot ceilings."

Millicent shook her head in wonder at their arcane knowledge of Christmas tree height. "The one thing I've undertaken on my own imagination is to order a snow machine that will create a gentle snowfall outside the two windows on either side of the fireplace. All the emphasis Sage has put on Aunt Pelipa's determination that this be an old-fashioned Christmas—right down to not letting me know when they're coming, as there are to be no phones—I thought that there's nothing that's a more vintage Christmas than a beautiful snowfall."

"*Oh ...*" Alison said, then paused.

"Don't tell me that's a bad idea," Millicent lamented.

"Not necessarily bad, but potentially more worry than you need, with all you have to take care of."

"Will it not be lovely and mood-invoking?"

"Yes, dear, it will surely be that."

"Well now, I don't know what to think. Anyway, the machine has been ordered and paid for, so, good or bad, there will be snow. Fake snow. *Hmmm*, I see. Aunt Pelipa might not think much of a fake snow. Well, then, let's put it this way, *I* want snow outside these two windows, and if no one else enjoys it, *I will!*"

"And I will, too, darling," Eric said. "I think it's a lovely idea, and it'll be a big surprise for everyone, other than the folks in this room."

"I'll love it too, Millicent. Don't take me wrong. I was just thinking about less work for you. Speaking of which, let's put the finishing touches to the decorations."

The four of them flitted about the mansion putting up swags and boughs and trinkets, and froufrou and candles until the night was well spent.

But when they were through, Sage's mansion had become an enchanting, old-fashioned, Christmas fairyland.

Chapter 5

Alison & Anthony

Finally, Alison and Eaton wended their way home the short distance to the neighboring mansion in the wee hours of the morning.

"Thank you, Eaton, for sticking it out with us. You've had quite the day of holiday decorating. Sleep in tomorrow … I mean, today…."

"Thank you, Miss Alison. I doubt that will be necessary. In any case, I quite enjoyed myself. Like old times."

"Yes," Alison said quietly, revealing a sadness she couldn't hide.

"*Ah!* Don't worry about Anthony. You know how he is. He gets his mind on a bit of business, and that's where it stays until he clears it up."

"True. Well, I just hope he 'clears it up', pronto. It won't do for him to be morose with two households full of company and Christmas joy."

"We will pull him from his doldrums if necessary."

"Yes, we will!" She smiled and gave a small wave as she climbed the grand stairway. When she entered the master suite, she was surprised to see Anthony wide awake, pacing the room.

He turned to her with a peculiar expression on his face that she had not seen before. "Where were you?"

"At Sage's with Eaton, helping Millicent and Eric put up Christmas decorations. Where, I might add, you could have been. Clara knew where we were, and I couldn't find you when we left. Quite frankly, the weird way you've behaved today, I wasn't sure you'd be particularly pleasant to have along. In any case, you could have called me."

"True. True, true, true. Weird behavior, unpleasant to be around … all true." He paced up and back across the room again.

Alison crossed the room to sit in the small slipper chair, watching him without the slightest inkling of what was going on. "Are you going to let me know what's up, or shall I go to another room while you sort out your demons?"

"My demons! Yes, well said. One demon, anyway. My greatest fear. I have only one."

"Only one fear! You have most of the human race beat on that score, I'd say. Would you care to share with me what that fear is?"

"No. That's the problem, I really, really, really do not want to have this talk. But I must."

Alison felt her heart begin to race. What could he possibly have to say that she knew nothing about, that would have this stalwart and resilient man in such a state?

"Anthony, please! Please just come over here and *sit* and *talk*. What you're doing now is not constructive."

"No. It's not." He sat on the edge of the bed, reaching out like he would take her hands, and then pulled back. He sighed deeply. "All right, then. My greatest fear is, of course, losing you, and …."

"*Losing me?*" Alison interrupted. "There's only one way you'd lose me!" She wanted to jump up, but she sat, frozen.

"*No! No, no, no*, Alison, it's not … that! But, it's well, you know, you have a life in San Francisco, and it would be easy for you to be there more than here, and for us to appear the same to everyone on the surface. Everyone is used to your coming and going. But here, in our inner sanctum … will what I'm about to say change that?"

Alison finally did stand, but more from exasperation, now, than fear. "Really, Anthony. The bush you're beating has been well thrashed. Will you *kindly* get to the point?"

"Yes. Well. Yes. So, this morning, while you and Eaton were getting the Christmas decorations out of the attic, I came up to help, and I got a phone call …."

"Goodness, Anthony, I'm well aware of that. Eaton is well aware of that. The attic rafters are well aware of that. You got a call, and right in the midst of our cheerful holiday banter, you threw a big bucket of ice water on us with your weird change in mood and subsequent disappearance."

"Oh. Yes. Of course. You … I did … I was … right. The phone call was from one of my attorneys …."

"Yes?"

"A couple weeks ago I'd called him to tell him to be sure to put some fairly recent acquisitions of mine in your name as well. Simple business, crossing t's, dotting i's. And I was shocked when he called and told me … well, you know how, in San Francisco, that night after your gallery opening, and we went to the ocean, and …."

"Yes, Anthony, I remember. That's why I'm back in this house. Do *you* remember? Goodness! What is going on with you?"

"So, okay, that night I confessed that I'd never filed our divorce papers, and that, technically, we were never divorced. To which you wisely responded, 'what if I'd gotten married again?' and, well, as I said, I was quite happy that you hadn't. So, anyway, the second happiest day of my life—the first one being when you agreed to marry me in the first place—the second happiest day of my life was that night when you agreed to return here and live with me."

He paused again. "But … it seems … that is, my attorney informed me that when he was setting up the paperwork I'd requested, and looked into the legal documents that entailed, he discovered that, in point of fact … in point of fact the other attorney that I'd instructed *not* to file the divorce papers, in fact, apparently did.

"Because, ahm, it seems, that … ahm … in point of fact, we are actually … not presently legally married."

Alison sighed what she thought was a sigh of relief. But then, no! This was too strange. On one hand, it seemed completely irrelevant. But on the other hand, somehow she felt betrayed. Why? She'd filled out the divorce papers. It was her intention at the time. But she didn't want to have to replay all that pain. She didn't want to have to even *think* about it.

And, further, she now understood Anthony's peculiar behavior, all day going through the same—or surely similar—thoughts such as she now processed.

Anthony raised his hands, pleading. "Say something, Alison. Please, say anything."

"Say anything? I'll begin by saying this certainly does explain your behavior today. And, given the unusual, bustling activities of the day, I can now understand why your odd behaviors were so especially … odd. You were processing this unexpected information. I was too busy with Eaton and Clara to get into this conversation. Then I was gone all evening. Almost all night. Okay. I can see how it might escalate to your present proportions. But, really, Anthony, *really*, it doesn't change anything. I mean, we're married in our hearts, and no, I'm not going to scurry back to live full-time in San Francisco because of a paperwork snafu.

"Goodness!" she exclaimed, her exasperation reaching its limit. "Do you really think my love is that paper-thin, this being, after all, a discussion of a mere piece of paper?"

Anthony hurried to her and took her hands in his. "Thank you, darling. Thank you. Of course!" He shrugged. "Don't I know who you are? I let my ego get in the way. The broken part of my ego. I do wish I could expunge him, but I fear we're both stuck with him for the duration.

"I can handle huge business deals where enormous concerns may rise and fall. But when it comes to you, darling of my heart, I'm ... not that person. It was such hell the years we were apart. And I spent the whole day, instead of being in the beautiful holiday spirit, imagining being without you again. *The horror of being without you again.* I let my thoughts run away with me."

"You certainly did! Well, let us move on from here and enjoy the season. Our precious Sage and Michael, and their entire entourage, which no one has any idea who or how many it will be—Millicent is in a small meltdown, and I don't blame her—will soon be here. Let us put our petty stuff aside and engage in what is actually important."

Anthony kissed Alison's fingers. "Of course. You always put things in reasonable perspective. Of course! I am so looking forward to Michael and Sage coming. Please forgive me for being a big old sullen toad on this, otherwise, beautiful day. I hoped and hoped our conversation would be something like this when we finally had it."

He stood and went around the bed to his bedside table, opened the drawer and removed something, then returned to Alison. "This was going to be one of your Christmas gifts, but now it's timely in another way." He got down on one knee before her and opened a small red velvet box, revealing a stunning, blue-tinted, diamond-shaped diamond. "Darling Alison, love of my life, will you marry me?"

Alison could not hide her surprise. "Oh! Anthony, it's beautiful! Truly breathtaking! But ... no, I'm not going to marry you. I mean, it's not necessary. We're married in essence. There's no need to make an issue of our private business that only concerns us. I love you. I'm happily relieved that the mountain you climbed today was merely a molehill."

She giggled. "And I could slap you for putting me through this day. Eaton, too, in fact. Poor guy. He was all stalwart and calm, like he is. But I know him. He was quite concerned. So, it's only fair to let him in on our strange kerfuffle. And Clara too, I imagine. Our lovely support team—what would we do without them?

"But, anyway, no, no need for a marriage ceremony."

"But, Alison, I … it … it doesn't feel right to me. I mean, I put you through hell and I just want us to be properly and legally married."

"No, sweetheart, I'll take the ring, but please put it away until Christmas morning. I'll act like I just did, astounded by its beauty. All's well that ends well." She leaned over and kissed him on the cheek. "Let's go to sleep. I'm beyond exhausted, it's been a very, *very* long day, physically and, thanks to you, emotionally draining. I need to sleep."

"Of course, of course. I'm such a clod. You need your beauty sleep. And so do I!"

Alison crossed the room to her dresser, taking off her jewelry and brushing her hair.

"But, Alison …."

"Yes, dear?"

"I'm serious—I want to marry you. Please, give it more thought."

Yawning, she shrugged her shoulders. "I hear you, dear. We'll see." Which, they both knew, was Alison-speak for "Probably not."

Chapter 6

The Snow Machine

The next morning, the first thing Millicent had to attend to was the snow machine. It arrived with three burly men who immediately got into the labor of setting it up outside, above the windows on either side of the fireplace. A complicated affair, requiring the building of a temporary scaffolding, and an advisement from the supervisor that "no one mess around under the scaffolding."

"Right," Millicent noted, "no 'messing around' under the snow machine," shaking her head. *As if!* No one would even be outside, and certainly not on this side of the mansion, in the trees, away from all entrances.

After four hours, which included much banging and hammering and dragging of equipment and components across the grass, leaving tracks that Millicent hoped Sage would not notice, and causing Emdee to become nearly apoplectic with barking and jumping at the windows, determined to protect her domain and mistress from the hulking creatures, the three mountain men came stomping through the front door without preamble. The supervisor handed

Millicent a remote control to initiate the fall of snow outside the windows.

They all crowded into the space in front of the fireplace. Millicent picked up Emdee, who had become even more beside herself with the invasion of the terrifying creatures into her very home. She pushed the button on the remote. Nothing happened. She pushed the button again. Again, nothing.

At that moment, Eric came through the front door and into the living room, having been at Anthony's tending to the horses. "I see," he said, taking in the three workers, "a truck in the driveway with 'Let it Snow' blazoned across its sides. So …." He looked out the window. "No snow."

"No," Millicent said bleakly, handing Emdee to Eric. "No snow."

"We'll be right back." The three men stomped through the house, out the front door, and were soon seen again under the windows. The supervisor began to yell at the other two, as if they could neither be seen nor heard by anyone.

Emdee growled.

"My sentiments, exactly," Millicent agreed. "They've been here for hours. They tore up the grass with all their lugging of stuff. They built a scaffolding." She looked down at the floor in front of the fireplace and took in the dirty tracks all the way to the front door. "They made tracks through my clean house. *Oh! I could cry.*"

"Don't cry. They're almost done. When they're gone, I'll clean their tracks up faster than you can think about it. And you'll have your beautiful snow."

There was a crashing sound, making them all jump and Emdee growl louder than Millicent thought such a small dog would even have the ability to growl. A long board fell across the window. Millicent frowned and shrugged. "Okay. I guess I can be grateful that that board didn't come *through* the window."

"One begins to wonder if these guys are competent," Eric mused.

"Oh, one left that wonder behind hours ago, and one has now come to the wonderment if it's possible that, given their incompetence, they'll be able to perform their job *at all*."

"I have faith. Even a blind pig finds an acorn once in a while."

"Yes. Blind pigs. Okay. Except I'm pretty certain that pigs, even blind ones, are more skillful."

They watched as the errant board was apparently, and hopefully, put back where it belonged. The yelling continued non-stop.

"Do you want me to go out and supervise the supervisor?" Eric asked. "You don't deserve to be subjected to this bad behavior."

"No. Since I can't hear what he's saying, it's all right. Anyway, I suspect that's the only way this team—if it can be called that—works."

Suddenly, silence fell. And then the three workers were making another path through the rooms, just in case they couldn't find their way with the previous one they'd laid down.

"I think it's good," the supervisor said. "This nut case here," he waved to one of his two peers, "forgot to flip the 'on' switch. We nearly lost the whole damn, sorry, ma'am, darn thing there for a minute, fussing around with the scaffolding."

"Yes. We witnessed the board falling. I was grateful that it did not come through the window."

"Me too, me too," he agreed. "Anyway, now, please, if you would try the remote."

Millicent had little hope of success as she pressed the 'gentle snow' button.

Tick-tock.

Emdee growled.

A gentle snow began to fall outside the two windows!

"It's … it's beautiful!" Millicent whispered.

Eric put Emdee down and wrapped his arm around Millicent. "It truly is. You were right. It creates a lovely holiday mood."

There was a slight waver in Eric's voice. She looked up at him.

"I didn't expect this … this feeling. It makes me feel like a child."

Emdee had scurried to the window, and though barely able to see out when extending herself her full length with her front paws on the window sill, augmented her throaty growl.

Millicent and Eric laughed. "Don't worry little dog, you needn't protect us from this strange, white invasion," Eric said.

Millicent pushed the button for 'medium snow' and the snowfall redoubled.

"There's something that will need to be cleaned up!" Eric said.

"No. It's some kind of soap bubbles," Millicent turned the snow back to "gentle." "Supposedly completely disappearing and environmentally friendly. Kinda like real snow!" She turned to the three workers, who seemed to be mesmerized in their own snow-watch.

"Thank you, gentlemen. Good job, we have snow!"

The supervisor shook himself out of his reverie. "Right! Come on, guys. We have two more snow machines to put up today, and I don't know how we're going to get it done."

"Thanks again." Millicent walked them to the front door, thinking, but not saying, *and please take your tracks with you.*

No need. As soon as she closed the door and turned, she saw Eric already with rag and cleaner in hand.

She came back into the living room.

"Just sit and watch your snow," he said, quickly working his way across the living room, and into the foyer.

"Don't mind if I do." She sat on the sofa. Emdee hurried to her and jumped into her lap, and they watched the gentle snow. Soon Eric joined them.

* *

After a few minutes of enjoying their quiet reverie, with even Emdee seeming to enjoy, rather than be threatened by, the snow, Millicent reached for the remote and shut it off. A few flakes wandered down, and then all was still.

"Wow! That's a feeling of power! *Let it snow! Let it stop!* It reminds me of Aunt Pelipa, when it seemed pretty obvious that she made it not rain on Sage and Michael's outdoor wedding."

Eric nodded. "Except I think she maybe has a different sort of remote control."

"Indeed!"

"*Soooo*, hating to shift this incredible moment. But, I think, if I'm not mistaken, we have a Christmas tree to find."

"We do. Although I don't like the idea of being responsible for taking the life of a tree, I believe this mansion has perhaps never had the beautiful ritual of a living tree indoors during the shift of the seasons, which the pagans honor. I'm trying to come to terms with it."

"I love you," Eric said, kissing her forehead. "We will find a tree that has been specifically grown to honor the holiday, and we'll make a pledge to plant a tree."

"Oh! Perfect. I love you too!" She jumped up. "Let's go!" She regarded Emdee on the sofa, looking expectantly from her to Eric as if she knew exactly what was going on. "Well, Little Miss, do you want to go with us?"

"*Woof!*" the little black dog said, running back and forth on the sofa. "*Woof-woof-woof!*"

"I think that's a yes." Eric said.

"Shall I put one of your Christmas sweaters on you?"

"*Woof!*" Emdee said.

"I'll be right back." Millicent went to the hall closet and soon returned with a red cozy crocheted sweater, covered in little white kittens.

"Where did you find such a cute sweater?"

"At *Love Your Pet Vet*. A woman crocheted darling sweaters for cats and dogs, even some for birds, that have kittens and puppies and birds on them. She's giving all the money from their sale to *Love Your Pet Vet*, and Dr. Davis is giving the money to the animal shelter."

"*Awww*, Millicent. That's very touching. I'll have to go buy a couple of creature sweaters!"

Millicent laughed. "And what will you do with them?"

"Give them to Miss Emdee, of course." He looked down at her. "Will you like that?"

"*Woof! Woof! Woof-woof-woof!*" Emdee barked at length and heartily.

"She likes it!"

Chapter 7

The Tree

The three of them climbed into Eric's truck and took off down the winding driveway. Emdee sat at attention on the seat, watching everything go by, while Millicent brought up on her phone a list of places to buy Christmas trees.

"There's one nearby." She gave him the address, but when they came to it, it looked small and a bit scruffy. So they continued on, farther out into the country. The day held warmth and sunshine, bathing everything in a friendly glow. Millicent was in a delicious mood, unable to imagine a more perfect outing than this one, with the man and the doggie she adored.

But then, the memory of Eric having proposed to her crowded into her mind. She'd kept this thought at bay, but now, such thoughts would not be stayed. However, just because she had the thoughts didn't mean she had any idea what to do with them. She still felt that "getting married"—*what a phrase!*—would rock their tidy, cozy boat. And she didn't want it rocked. Not at all. Not in the least, tiny, little bit.

But she found herself looking over at him, as he hummed some tune quietly to himself—another adorable feature among his plethora of adorable features, he had a beautiful singing voice—and she could not stop musing the thought of actually having this person as her husband.

Hmmm … Difficult to picture. Hard to put down.

He glanced over at her. "What's going on in that beautiful head of yours?"

"Nothing. Much."

"I doubt it. Always something going on. But the noise of your silence is about to break the sound barrier."

"Oh. Sorry. All right. I'll silence my silence."

They both laughed and fell back into their companionable quiet.

"Here we are at the tree farm you turned up. Looks pretty good."

Millicent took in the rows and rows of still living trees, and the few near the roadside that had been cut. They looked strong and green and lovely. "I think this is the place."

Eric pulled into the crowded parking lot—only a couple days until Christmas, and everyone without a tree had apparently decided to come to this very place. Millicent put a harness on Emdee over her kitty sweater and clipped a leash to the harness. "Let's go!"

They moved into the throng of tree shoppers. A crowd like this usually put Millicent very much on edge, but the mood was altogether festive, and everyone chatted as if they were one big family. There seemed to be enough trees to go around, and happy, smiling families, young couples, and older couples, were tying trees to the tops of their cars or putting them in the backs of trucks, with help from the tree farm employees, everyone jovial and pleasant.

"*So nice!*" Millicent whispered to Eric. "Can strangers really get together like this and be so nice?"

"They can. The employees are setting the tone. And all the customers are happy to share it."

They wandered among the wonderland of trees, moving farther into the rows, as the trees were graduated in size, searching for the perfect, tall tree.

There were plenty of other dogs there as well. Emdee appeared to be at her height of happiness as she came nose to nose with a few of them. Whether large or small, it didn't matter. They were all dogs. And that made them pals.

Millicent didn't know exactly what she was looking for. She hoped Eric would take over—she felt certain he'd know the right tree when he saw it.

But then she looked to her left and suddenly she saw it. *THE TREE*. It practically spoke to her: *"I am the tree which you seek."*

"Here, Eric. This one." She pulled Emdee and Eric over to the majestic, perfect tree. "Is it good? It just … it seems right."

"It's gorgeous, Millicent. Good eye. Yes, I believe this is our tree."

Emdee sniffed at a low branch.

"Do you like this tree, Emdee?"

"Woof! Woof-woof!" she agreed.

"Done, then," Millicent said. "Now what?"

"Now we pay for it. We have one of the employees help me get it in the truck and make sure it's properly tied down. Then we get a sturdy tree stand because this is a big and heavy tree. And we see if maybe they have a few more ornaments, which I think we'll need, because it's not only tall, but it's wide in girth."

"Oh! The project expands! Let's get at it."

Before long the tree was in the back of Eric's truck, he and the employee chose a massive tree stand that they agreed the tree needed. Finally, they went inside the festive little shop. It was toasty and smelled of ginger and apple cider. And for good reason, as women in elf costumes served cups of steaming apple cider along with plates of brightly decorated cookies.

Millicent handed Emdee's leash over to Eric and gathered up strings of tree lights, some darling rocking horse ornaments, reminiscent of the large ones in front of the house, three or four boxes of sparkling ornaments, handmade chocolates, and giant, sliced, candied fruits.

Then she found a beautiful, silver sparkling tree skirt—another thing that had not crossed her mind. The little shopping cart she'd finally conceded to getting became full to over-flowing.

Eric stood by with Emdee, sipping apple cider. The little dog happily wagged her tail, taking in all the activity. People stooped over to tell her how cute she was, which she completely lapped up—but her eyes were continually on Millicent.

Finally, Eric wandered over to her. "Are you buying the whole little shop?" he teased.

Millicent looked at her shopping cart, a bit surprised. "Oh, dear! Too much?"

"I don't think so. It's a big tree, and there'll be lots of people in the house, so all the chocolates and candied fruit will be much appreciated."

"Oh, no! I completely forgot! Tina and John are coming over today to bring goodies to put in the freezer and wherever else they have to put them." She looked at her watch. "We'd better go. But I don't know when I've had so much fun spending Sage's money."

"And Sage's money has never had so much fun being spent!" Eric chuckled. "All righty, let's get this loot in the truck. Putting up the tree and decorating it is a bit of a project, too."

"Again, without thought about details! What would I do without you?"

"Let's never find out."

Soon they had piled all their "loot" in the truck, headed for tree mounting and decorating.

Chapter 8

Trims & Treats

They soon arrived back at the mansion. Eric found a tarp in the garage and the two of them carefully pulled the tree off the truck bed, onto the tarp, through the double-wide front door, and through the house to the fireplace.

"Where do you want it to stand?" Eric asked after bringing in the tree stand.

"I thought right about here," Millicent said, standing to the side of the left fireplace window. "But it's so big I think it'll cover the window, and thus, the snow. After all the fuss about snow!"

"You're right. This tree will entirely cover the window if we stand it where you're standing. It can go farther over to the left, I think. It's still not in the way of anything and will let people move around it. And, most importantly, it leaves the window almost entirely visible."

"Excellent. Let's do it. But … *how* do we do it? It's really heavy."

"I just need you to be sure the base of the trunk is aligned with the tree stand when I lift the tree. I'm sorry that you'll be in the thick of the branches, but you needn't do any lifting."

"You're going to lift the tree by yourself?"

"Sure, it's not that heavy. Ready?"

Millicent eyeballed the tree stand and the tree trunk. "All right. I'm ready if you are."

Eric hoisted the tree to standing. Sure enough, she was completely enwrapped in tree branches, but she kept her focus on the trunk and the tree stand, directing the trunk into the stand. It slid neatly into place.

Millicent extricated herself from the branches and surveyed their handiwork, so thrilled with the beauty of the gigantic tree standing tall that she clapped like a little child. "Beautiful, Eric, just *beautiful!*"

"It's very beautiful. Like you. Well," he put his arm around her. "Not exactly like you, because it's a tree, and you're a beautiful woman."

"Oh, stop it. You know what I think of talk like that. I'm not beautiful. I do sometimes think I've discovered how to make myself a bit pretty, but beauty is beyond my range."

"And we will, my precious, continue to agree to disagree on the subject. You'll not change my mind. But I do wish you could see the you *I* see."

"Maybe I do, too. And maybe it would ... frighten me."

"Frighten you! Why would that be?"

"Well, if you have a picture of yourself in your mind's eye. and you suddenly see yourself as looking entirely different, even if that was objectively more physically attractive, wouldn't it be unnerving to not look like one's self?"

"Yes. Probably."

"The thing is, in my family, my younger sister, Stephanie, is the beautiful one. I was the provider, the parent, when we were suddenly parentless. I didn't need to be pretty, I needed to take care of three siblings. Stephanie, the beauty, Peter, the boy, and Baby, our little sister. Pretty was not a commodity I needed."

"Perhaps not. But pretty is an attribute you have. And anyway, my pet, it's all irrelevant because once I got to know you, I fell in love with the beauty of the person you are. And even though you are a delicate beauty, that's not nearly as important to me as the sweet, loving, caring, giving, *amazing being* you are."

"Stop, stop, stop, please. Okay, don't stop. The 'loving, caring, giving' part I appreciate. I hope I am. But, now, getting back to the tree!"

"Yes. The tree. We need to water it. I'll do that while you get the sparkly tree skirt you so cleverly bought, which, frankly, I forgot about. And we'll soon have the prettiest tree in the neighborhood."

"Given that the closest neighbors are Anthony and Alison, and they're a mile-and-a-half away, I'd say we're the *only* Christmas tree in the neighborhood."

"Umm, yes, that too."

Eric brought the six-foot ladder in from the garage, then they gathered all the lights and ornaments for the tree. With considerable 'help' from Emdee who thought that their actions were the most exciting she'd ever seen, dancing about them, yipping, and generally getting underfoot, they launched into decorating the enormous tree, Millicent handing lights up to Eric, as they worked their way around and down the tree.

Even with Millicent having practically bought out the little tree shop of its lights, along with the ones they'd bought the previous day, they were still shy enough lights.

"We'll have to redo some of the lights," Eric said. "I'll take down a couple of the strings, and bring them more to the front. The back of the tree is against the wall, so no one will notice."

"I was wondering what to do about this vast terrain of darkness," Millicent said, waving her hand around the unlit footage of the tree.

When they were satisfied with the bright and even distribution of the lights, they began hanging the ornaments.

"I always wondered," Millicent said, "since I could never afford a tree, if it was lights first, then ornaments, or ornaments then lights."

"Lights first! If you hang ornaments first, they're getting knocked off the tree when putting on the lights."

"Yes. I see that now … quite the learning curve. Next …."

The front door chimes rang throughout the mansion.

"That must be Tina and John."

At the front door, Tina and John stood hovering over a cart laden with delicacies four feet high.

"Come in, come in—oh, my goodness! What all have you brought us?"

"Ten of everything!" Tina exclaimed.

"*Wonderful!* The kitchen and pantry are yours. Do as you will. Eric and I are decorating the tree, the first time I've done it in my life."

"*Whoa!*" John exclaimed. "Now *there's* a tree!"

"Is it big enough?" Tina quipped.

Millicent frowned. "Is it too big?"

"No. I'm teasing," Tina winked. "It's perfect in that space. Anything smaller and it would look a bit unintentional."

"While this tree is clearly intentional," John said.

"And," Tina carried on, "you can make a cabin from the wood when the holidays are over."

"All right, you guys, stop dissing our tree," Eric defended, coming down from the ladder. "Instead, kindly feed me something from your vast wares." He surveyed the array of delicacies. "Speaking of overkill!"

"Oh, no, Eric!" Millicent cried. "We haven't eaten all day. Why didn't you say something? You know I don't eat unless fed. Those cookies at the tree farm were enough for me. Especially with my mind on the tree … I'm hopeless!"

"No, you're not. I'm an adult, you don't need to feed me. I'm much more fond of the notion of feeding you. But now we have this wealth of food right in front of us, and I don't see why we can't both feed ourselves. Time for a break from tree business!"

While Tina and John put the canapés, petit fours, bonbons, cakes, savories, chocolates, so on and so forth, in various refrigerator, freezer, pantry spaces, Millicent and Eric helped them with their chore by diminishing the product.

"I can't rave enough about how out-of-this-world every single thing is. There isn't anything I didn't like," Millicent said as John wheeled the cart to the front door.

"I'm relieved to hear it, although I'd be surprised to hear otherwise." Tina grinned. "We get five-star reviews from everyone, don't we my love?"

"We do," John agreed. "Nary a four-star review, not a one. Well, we gotta get back to the kitchen. We'll have another delivery tomorrow, not ready yet. We'll be up almost all night."

"Oh!" Millicent exclaimed, "I don't like to hear that!"

"We love it. We get a kick out of pulling an all-nighter—we get into a zone. We're both night owls, and our creative juices flow after the world goes to sleep."

Millicent opened the door and John pushed the cart through. "In that case, have a lovely, creative night. See you tomorrow!"

Tina, waving over her head, helped John roll their cart up into the van.

Millicent returned to the tree and watched as Eric hung the last three ornaments in their possession. They stood back to admire their handiwork.

"I really do think it's the most beautiful tree in the world. And it smells of the forest. Heavenly!" Millicent said in a hushed voice.

"It is. It does."

"Even if there aren't very many lights on the back."

"Doesn't matter. Thank you, beautiful tree."

"Yes," Millicent agreed. "Thank you, amazing tree. Oh! I nearly forgot, I've got presents to put under the tree. It'll look more homey with presents, won't it?"

"It will."

"I'm so glad I've been getting presents all along, because, well, because I don't have to go shopping at the last minute, which I simply couldn't now, anyway.

And because it will give the tree a finished look. Don't go anywhere."

"Hadn't planned on it."

Millicent scurried to the office and pulled out a pile of presents from the closet, wrapped and ready to go under the tree. She bumped into Eric as she came out of the office.

"*Oh!* I said, 'don't go anywhere.'"

"I thought that was figurative and you could use some help." He took the top three presents from her pile.

"That *is* helpful—I can see where I'm going now."

They returned to the tree and placed her presents under it.

Millicent stepped back and studied the effect. "Oh, dear, it doesn't look right, does it? They're lost under that huge tree. It's almost better without the presents. This just looks kinda sad. And ...." she paused, "there's something wrong. I can't quite figure it, but what's missing?"

"*Oh!*" Eric whispered with insight. "I know what it is, and I can't believe I forgot."

"What? What is it, Eric?"

He pointed to the top of the tree.

"*Ohhh!*" Millicent gasped. "We don't have an angel for the top of the tree! How could we have forgotten her?"

"I don't know. But it's not a disaster. It's just an oversight. We can perhaps take one of the ornaments and put it up there."

"None of the ornaments are ...."

At that moment, the front door chimes echoed through the mansion.

"Who could that be? I'm not expecting anyone or anything. And, I really don't want to have to *deal* with anyone or anything right now. I'm dealing with the missing angel crisis."

"Not a crisis, Millicent. But do you want me to dispatch whoever is at the door? It's probably a lost delivery person, as it's only a couple days before Christmas, and there's plenty of deliveries being made."

The chimes rang again. "No, I'll get it." Resigned, Millicent dragged her feet to the front door.

"*Surprise!*" Sage cried, giving Millicent a big hug.

Chapter 9

Surprise!

It was, indeed, a surprise!

"I didn't think you were coming until tomorrow, at the earliest," Millicent said, adding the distress of how far she was from being ready for Sage and Michael to be here to the upset about no angel for the tree.

"I told Michael it wasn't fair to you—despite Aunt Pelipa's decree for no phones and an old-fashioned Christmas—to feel you have to have the place pulled together, not knowing when people were coming, nor how many. But I knew if I told you we were coming a bit early, you'd try to have everything done before I got here, and I didn't want you to do that.

"In other words, we're here to help!"

"But … where's Michael?" Millicent asked.

"I think he's reminiscing with the children on horse figures. He was quite moved to see them."

"Oh! How sweet! Alison and Eaton brought them over, along with a couple of boxes of smaller Christmas memories." If Michael was emotional over the yard decorations, Millicent thought, what would he experience when he saw his little bears and the snow globe?

Michael came to the door, while at the same time, Eric had come down from the ladder and joined them.

"*Sage! Michael!*" Eric exclaimed.

"*Ricky!*" Michael gave his lifelong friend a giant hug. He then turned to Millicent. "My little friend, how glowing and beautiful you are!"

Emdee had awakened from her nap and joined them, leaping about as if she would come right out of her hide with joy. Sage stooped over and picked the little dog up, while Michael enveloped Millicent in a hug. She felt a fleeting feeling for him that she'd felt for years. But it was only fleeting. He was Michael. He would always be Michael. But ... *he is not Eric* her heart told her.

So true! she told her heart. "Well, come on in. You're right, Sage, I'm feeling distressed that you're here and the place is nowhere ready for you! Eric and I have been fussing with a tree most of the day." They came into the living room. "And now, as you can see, there's light and ornament boxes everywhere, the ladder is still at the tree. And everything is just a mess, I'm sorry to say."

"Oh, Millicent, it's all lovely, and it smells fantastic, like Christmas. I *love* the disarray, the ladder ... the empty ornament and light boxes ... sweeter than sweet."

"You can thank Eric, who made gingerbread last night, and the wonderful evergreen tree, and Tina and John for the fantastic combined Christmas aromas. By the way, you just missed Tina and John."

"Oh! I'm sorry to have missed them!"

"They'll be back tomorrow. They said they'll be pulling an all-nighter to get everything to us that I ordered. I probably ordered too much, but, as you've already pointed out, I don't know how many people to plan on."

"What would I do without you?" Sage put her arm around Millicent. "It will all be fine. It all *is* fine! Michael and Eric, why don't you two go out and start to bring in the presents from the car, while Millicent and the adorable doggie and I sit here admiring the tree."

"We're on it!" The two men rushed off like small boys on a fun mission.

Sage sat, still holding Emdee, and patted the sofa beside her for Millicent to join her.

Millicent sat, but on the edge of the sofa. There was so much she had to do, how could she just sit and chat?

"Relax, dear Millicent. I am so, so, *so* very pleased with … well, with everything. The tree is breathtaking! I did not expect it, thank you!"

"But … but … Eric and I were just processing the disaster of forgetting to get an angel for the top of the tree when you came to the door."

Sage's small, calm smile grew. "Nothing to worry about."

"But it's not right. It's not … old-fashioned."

The two men came in, both completely laden with boxes, large and small.

"I told you it wouldn't take long for the tree to look well-populated!" Eric grinned over the stack of brightly colored packages.

Sage leapt up and started taking them from him and placing them under the tree.

"Millicent," Michael called from behind an even larger pile, "*Help!*"

"Gladly!" She laughed, despite her worries. She felt them slipping away in the billowing joy among her friends. If they were happy, she was happy! She grabbed the top, smaller boxes Michael carried and placed them under the tree. She even let go—a little bit—of concerning herself with how each box was placed.

Sage was giggling and putting the presents willy-nilly, joining in the child-like enthusiasm of Michael and Eric. "Is that everything?"

"Not quite. But nearly so."

"Bring them on!" she ordered.

Soon, yet more presents spilled out from under the tree as if the tree itself had manifested them. Eric had set the ladder aside while the melee of fun ensued.

"I'll take the ladder back out to the garage, now," he said.

"Not quite just yet," Sage stayed his hand.

"Oh? All right."

"Let's go upstairs," Sage said, heading for the grand stairway.

Millicent exchanged a look with Eric. She feared that Sage was going to get the sad, broken decorations that had prompted them to spend much of the previous day buying new ones. Eric immediately understood her meaning. And they hadn't even yet gotten around to putting the awful boxes away, so there they stood, in the hall.

"Oh, Sage, I really haven't finished upstairs yet. Just let me have a few minutes …."

Hopeless! Sage was already two-thirds of the way up the stairs, with Michael one step behind her, and, as Millicent knew, they would not now be dissuaded.

"Doesn't matter," Sage called down.

Millicent and Eric hurried up after her. "If you're thinking about getting out Christmas decorations from the attic," Millicent panted as she reached Sage, who stood on the landing waiting for them, "Eric and I got them out yesterday, and I'm sad to say, they are not in good shape."

"Decorations from the attic?"

Millicent gestured down the hall where the three wretched boxes stood.

"Hmmm …" Sage shrugged and shook her head. "I don't know anything about those boxes. I've never had anything of mine in the attic. I always kept everything in my own safe place, because Aunt Victoria was forever rifling through my things, and throwing away things she didn't like. I learned young to hide my treasures.

"Now, Millicent, I'm going to show you my most secret hiding spot, if you promise never to throw away anything that is in it."

"Oh, Sage, more than promise. I would never—and *have* never—thrown away a single thing from this house other than, you know, trash."

"Very well." Sage led them down the hall to the linen closet. She opened the door and the fresh scent of clean linens poured out. Getting down on her knees, she pulled out a flat sheet of white plastic on the floor of the closet, upon which were neatly folded sheets. She reached even father into the space and pulled out a rectangle of sheetrock. Then she pulled out two plastic shoeboxes.

"My love!" Michael whispered. "Your sacred space!" He sat down on the floor beside her.

Sage nodded. She gestured Millicent and Eric to sit on the floor with them. "I got so tired of my most precious things disappearing. Then, one day, when I was in the hall bathroom, I noticed that the wall of the bathroom seemed to be farther into the room than the back of the linen closet. I tapped around on it and it also sounded hollow. So when Aunt Victoria went on one of her many trips, I got a hack saw and carefully cut this hole in the sheetrock. It took me practically all day. And I was right. There's over a foot of space between the linen closet wall and the bathroom wall.

"My biggest problem was that there was no floor in it, and I'm sorry to say that there is a little hacksaw somewhere down on the ground level, when I accidentally dropped it, trying to see where the bottom of this space is. So I then found a bit of wood in the garage and fashioned a floor, gathered my most precious things that I thought Aunt Victoria was likely to take and stuck them in these shoeboxes."

Sage slowly opened the top box. In it were trinkets, costume jewelry, little glass elves, and fairies. "Aunt Victoria hated anything that wasn't 'real.' Costume jewelry, which I loved. I didn't care if it was 'real' or not. If I found it pretty, that's all that I cared about. And then, I've always loved fairies and their compatriots. And, of course …." She opened the other shoebox and pulled out a paper sack," Angels."

She carefully pulled the sack off the most beautiful angel Millicent had ever seen.

"Oh, Sage. She is *so beautiful!*"

Sage nodded. "And she was always meant to go on a tree. But she has never been anywhere near one, only this dark space, hoping that this day would come. And even if she didn't wonder if this day would come, *I did*." She handed the angel to Millicent. "Here is your Christmas tree angel, Millicent."

"Oh, Sage, I'm so moved! But, of course, either you or Michael must put her on the tree. This is your first Christmas together, and that will be your first Christmas ritual." She watched as Sage began to put everything back as it was.

"You know, you needn't put your treasures hidden away anymore, Sage. They can be—wherever you want them!"

"You're right, Millicent. why not have them where I can enjoy them!" She closed up the secret hidey-hole, returned the sheets to their place, picked up the two plastic shoe boxes, and they all stood.

"I will put them in my room, where they belong."

They wandered down the hall to Sage and Michael's room. Millicent felt like she might be invading a private moment when Michael saw his bears and the snow globe. But, at the same time, she really, *really* wanted to be there.

When they all crowded into the room, Michael had his attention on Sage, and where she might put her childhood precious little things.

She went straight for the dresser, and then exclaimed, "Michael! Look! *Your bears!*"

"My bears?"

Millicent watched as he took in the charming row of bears. "My bears! *Oh! Millicent!*" He turned to her, surprised.

"Alison brought them over with some other ornaments, and the big candy canes and children on horses outside. She thought you would enjoy them."

"More than enjoy. Much more than enjoy!" Emotion threatened to take his voice.

"And we thought you might be happy to see this, as well." She gestured to the snow globe on the bedside table. Sage and Michael had to turn to see what she pointed at.

"*Oh, Michael!*" Sage whispered.

He moved to sit on the bedside, looking in wonder at the snow globe as if he couldn't believe his eyes. "I haven't seen this in years and *years!*"

"Alison told me," Millicent said, matching the hushed tones of Sage and Michael, coming to kneel before Michael on the floor, "about that one Christmas, when you were a small boy you turned to her and said, 'this is very important. This baby represents love. The round globe is like the earth, and the snow is like love and the baby is bringing love to earth.'"

"Michael!" Sage's voice caught. She sat by him on the bed. "How I love you!"

Millicent got up and moved to stand by Eric, still in the doorway. "You are too amazing," he whispered in her ear.

She shook her head no. "I'm only a stagehand, behind the scene."

"And *what* an important stagehand!"

*   *

They eventually wound their way back downstairs. Eric opened the ladder and placed it close to the tree. Then Michael climbed the ladder and put the beautiful angel atop the tree.

"Oh, wait a minute!" Millicent hurried to the back office and returned with her phone. "Aunt Pelipa may disapprove, but this is a moment that must be photographed. I'm sorry I don't have an antique Kodak camera, but this moment must be preserved."

She went snap-happy, taking dozens of pictures of Michael putting the angel in place, Sage and Michael under the tree, Eric and Michael by the tree, Sage and Michael and Eric by the tree, Emdee in many of the pictures, just because she was running around in such delight.

Eric finally said, "The moment is not duly recorded, Millicent, until you are in some of the pictures!"

"No, no! I don't want to be in the pictures. I can't stand to see myself in pictures!"

"You might be surprised. Anyway, doesn't matter, we want you in our pictures."

"Yes, yes," Michael and Sage chorused.

"I won't be happy until you're in a few pictures," Sage cajoled. "You did say you wanted me to be happy."

"*Arg!* I didn't know that included my pride! I can't *stand* how I look in pictures."

"And me, too," Michael insisted. "I won't be happy with a bunch of pictures of this special moment in all our lives, without you in the commemorating pictures."

"Oh, all right!" she handed her phone to Eric to snap pictures of them, then he handed it over to Michael, who snapped off a dozen, and he then gave the phone to Sage, who did the same.

"*Let's look!*"

They all crowded around Sage, who scrolled backward through the shots. Millicent was stunned to silence to see this very pretty, tiny, woman in the midst of three giant, gorgeous, god-like beings, surrounded by a veil of love from them all, with a little black dog dancing and twirling among them. What a happy, if demure, expression of love on the features of this lovely little woman.

"That's me?" she whispered, sincerely bemused.

"I told you," Eric said, holding her close.

"Beautiful pictures, every single one," Sage declared. "Be sure to send them to us."

"I will, of course." She couldn't even think of all she had to do yet, she was so mystified by the unrecognizable person who smiled back at her in the pictures.

Sage yawned. "Let's get the ladder into the garage and clear up the boxes and such. It's been a long day, with lots to do tomorrow. I'm ready for some sleep."

Everyone muttered their agreement and soon the only sound to be heard was the ticking of the grandfather clock.

Chapter 10

Christmas Eve Eve – Morning

Millicent was up the next morning long before anyone else. She wandered outside with Emdee and took a much-needed walk. Emdee was delighted—she needed a walk too! When they'd ambled some distance from the mansion, Millicent turned and looked at it, thinking about how it held the people who were most dear to her, along with the neighboring home, where, no doubt, Alison and Anthony still slept, and also, of course, her siblings. But they were together in some small town in the state of Washington, not so far away. And yet, *so far away*.

Well, sometime on Christmas day she'd slip away from everyone, go to her room and have a nice long chat with them. Sighing deeply, surprised that she missed them so, she resolved to send them pictures of "her" Christmas tree. She'd already mailed them presents a week ago. Now that she had money, she spent what she could on expensive gifts, even though Stephanie, a young adult woman herself, told her such indulgences were not necessary.

Not necessary. Of course not necessary! But the presents gave her pleasure. During their childhood she could never give them gifts, it was all she could do to keep the four of them together without CPS finding they were un-parented, and putting them in various foster homes.

She looked down the hill at Anthony's "castle" as she initially called it. She saw one little light come on—in the kitchen. There was Clara, baking up a storm for the holidays, when, still, they didn't know how many people were coming.

Odd how, even though that ought to frustrate her, she found it exciting. Aunt Pelipa was right. Who was going to come? When were they going to come? The anticipation was tantalizing.

There'll be Aunt Pelipa and Uncle Halian. There'd be Sage's four younger cousins, Lolotea, Sunitha, and their brothers, the twins, Lonan and Lusio. Alison and Anthony with Clara and Eaton would come over tomorrow, or perhaps even today. She forgot to ask Sage if they told Alison and Anthony they were here. But she suspected that she hadn't as she didn't mention it.

Well! It was Christmas Eve Eve, and she had much to do, she was certain. Although what? Everything was much done. Other people were cooking—thank goodness, very much *not* her strong point. The tree was up, with presents spilling out into the surrounding area. Sage and Michael were perfectly happy with their accommodations, and anything else Sage wanted, it was her home, and she knew where to find it.

She headed for the back door, Emdee trotting alongside her, joyfully chatting in her little doggie way. Yes. The little, four-legged "person" made her life complete.

"Are you happy, my friend?"

"*Woof! Woof-woof!*" Emdee said.

"Me too! *Woof-woof!*" She swooped her little friend up and hugged her close, then slipped through the door. She heard clanging of cookware in the kitchen and was surprised to see Michael at work, getting out the waffle iron.

"Oh! I didn't expect to see you. Isn't it a bit early?"

"It's six a.m. on Christmas Eve Eve, and this boy needs to be fortified for a busy day. Eric mentioned his waffle-making, and I thought, *I can do that*. So, I'm making waffles."

"It's six a.m.? Was I outside that long? I went out at five, communing with nature and my little dog, enjoying the pending dawn, and thinking about who-all will likely turn up. Then I got to thinking about what I have to do, but couldn't quite sort that out. A lot is done, but there's always something that has been forgotten."

Michael nodded. "*I* don't even know when everyone's coming. They're driving. They're coming. That's all I know."

The front door chimes rang. "Certainly that's not them now," Millicent felt her heart jump into her throat. No. They were not supposed to come before tomorrow!

"I very much doubt it," Michael called as she headed for the door.

She opened it to Clara and Alison and Anthony. At the same time, she saw Eric's truck pull up behind their car, back from taking care of Anthony's horses.

"Clara just told us she saw Michael and Sage's car here!" Alison cried.

"Come in, come in," Millicent waved them in, relieved it was not a houseful of Sage's relatives. Not until tomorrow, please, she prayed. Eric came along behind them.

"I saw them leaving and followed them over," he leaned over and whispered to her. "I thought I'd make some breakfast."

"Believe it or not, Michael has a start on it, with the waffle iron out, and everything."

Eric raised his eyebrows in surprise.

"Uncle Anthony, Aunt Alison," Michael cried, abandoning the kitchen and rushing to them, with many resulting hugs.

Sage, in a flowing, Christmas green floor-length silk dressing gown, with her waist-length blond hair in a long braid over her shoulder, sailed into the kitchen. "You're here! I didn't want to bother you until later …."

"I saw your car when I got up to bake some more bread," Clara said. "I knew I'd be in trouble if I didn't tell the master right away."

"Nonsense," Anthony laughed. "But I'm glad you did."

"We're all glad you did," Alison stopped hugging Michael and went to hug Sage.

"Me too," Sage agreed. "It really didn't feel right not seeing you right away. But we were exhausted from the drive when we got in yesterday, and then we had a few things to do here."

"We're all together now, and that's all that matters," Anthony put his arm around Alison.

"So very true." Alison agreed.

"All right everyone," Eric announced, returning to the kitchen. "Go find a cozy place to sit where you'd like to be served breakfast, and I, and my talented sous chef, Mr. Michael, here …."

Michael took a deep bow.

"….will bring you a breakfast you'll long remember."

Everyone moved to the dining room table, which provided a wonderful view of the Christmas tree. Millicent was just a tiny bit tempted to turn on her snow machine. But no. The whole point of it was to make Christmas Eve truly special, and it would wait until tomorrow evening. Although she'd hoped to have a moment to test it today, just to make sure that it still worked. It seemed unlikely everyone would leave and let her work on her own projects.

The aroma of spiced tea and waffles rose up around them, making the gathering even more convivial.

"What shall we do today?" Sage asked. "Anything in particular, or nothing in particular?"

"It's such perfect weather, would it not be wonderful to go for a ride?" Alison suggested.

"I love it!" Sage exclaimed. "I was going to suggest it myself, but I didn't want to, if no one else felt like it."

"Anthony and I are always up for a ride!" Alison added.

"You can count me in," Michael said, intent on pouring batter in the waffle iron.

"I wouldn't even mind a bit of a ride myself," Clara said, still hovering around the table. "Oh, jeez, I got so excited about seeing Sage and Michael that I forgot to bring in my bread. I've got half-a-dozen-loaves in the car!" She scurried out the front door.

Everyone turned to look at Millicent.

"Why is everyone looking at me?"

"Because you're the only one who hasn't said you'll join us."

"Oh, well, I've got a lot to do here." She'd hoped she could be the quiet mouse, left alone to putter around the place and practice playing with her snow machine.

"Not so much to do," Eric argued, "that you can't go for a ride with us for a couple hours. It'll do you good. You've been stirring around in this place, putting it together for the holidays for a couple weeks. You've done a great job. Now, come play with us!"

"Play with us, play with us, play with us," Michael started to chant. Sage immediately joined in, and then they all were chanting, teasing her.

Clara came through the door carrying her wonderful loaves of bread. "For heaven's sake, girl, play with them! If I'm going to, and I have to make this much more bread, then you're going to!"

"All right, all right!" Millicent looked to see if she might be able to crawl under the dining room's oriental carpet. Embarrassed? Yes, hugely, but at the same time, her heart tripping with joy.

To heck with the snow machine! It would work. Anyway, that was a thought for tomorrow.

* *

The amazing breakfast, the convivial company, the little black dog, the stunning morning, all passed in an unforgettable tableau. Soon everyone went off to change into riding clothes. Millicent had even bought herself a proper riding habit, which she'd worn but once, all alone one day when she slipped over to Anthony's stables and took a wild ride on Thor.

But it had been too long, she was the first to agree, since she'd had the wind blowing through her hair on horseback, and she had to admit that, although not found in her little book of plans, this was the best plan of all.

Alison, Anthony, and Clara had hurried back home after the leisurely breakfast, with Eric following them, as he needed to put together all the tack, horse blankets, and saddles they'd need.

"Sorry you won't get to ride Thor," he said as he left. They both knew Thor was her favorite ride, but he was Anthony's horse.

"I don't mind." Millicent ran through in her mind which horse she'd likely be riding. One of the new ones she figured, as Twinkle was Alison's, Magenta was Sage's, and Michael would ride Scarlet.

There would be seven riders.

"Oh!" Eric said. "Solstice! Solstice is perfect for you. You haven't met her yet. She's a beautiful nearly black roan, with silver dappling. Quite striking! She was born three years ago on winter solstice. She's been beautifully trained and is a really nice mount. She's sweet, but has some spunk. Okay, gotta get over there and poke through the tack. We haven't had seven riders in quite a while." He looked hard at her for a moment, then said, "I'm so happy!" He kissed her.

"I'm happy too, dearest." She watched him walk to his truck—a sight she'd loved from the first and was certain she'd never find uninteresting. Then she finally closed the door and hurried upstairs to change. The riding getup still required her to give it thought to get into. The boots were downstairs in the front hall closet. When finally ready, she headed downstairs in her stocking feet. Disconcertingly, Sage and Michael were at the bottom of the stairs, watching her.

"Absolutely perfect!" Sage said. "You wear it well."

"True!" Michael agreed.

"Oh dear. Sorry to keep you waiting! I'm still a bit slow getting into this outfit."

"No problem. We just now came down ourselves. Are you ready?"

"Yes. Aside from the hassle of putting on the boots." She got them out of the closet.

"Michael will help you."

"Of course," Michael said. "Sit here." Michael helped her tug the riding boots on. She found it very interesting to realize that she felt nothing other than friendship. No strange little rushes, despite the fact that pulling on the boots was fairly personal.

The second boot on, she stood.

"Good?" Michael asked.

"Yes! I'm ready!"

She put Emdee in the back office with food, water, and her little bed, where she was content to be when alone as it had been her first home when she first came into Millicent's life. The little dog under horse's feet was something Millicent did not want to risk.

The three of them climbed into Sage and Michael's car and drove to the neighboring mansion, a ridiculously short drive, but they agreed that, although it would have been a nice walk, they wanted to spend their time on horseback.

Chapter 11

Christmas Eve Eve – Afternoon

They climbed out of the car. Seeing everyone at the stables, they hurried to join them.

"We'll be eight!" Anthony called. "Eaton is riding with us."

"That's special," Michael said, warmly shaking Eaton's hand. "It's so good to see you, Eaton."

"And you, as well, Michael," Eaton said. "I haven't ridden in a while, but I decided if everyone was going, I may as well go too. Hoping I stay astride my mount."

"We will all stay astride our mounts," Anthony ordered.

"Yes, sir," Alison responded, saluting him, while everyone chuckled.

"Such a beautiful array of horseflesh," Sage noted. "Who is that beauty, over there?" she pointed.

"That's Solstice," Eric said. "She was born on winter solstice three years ago, so she just had her third birthday."

"I hope she got some cake!"

"I did have treats for her. I thought she'd be a good mount for Millicent."

Millicent went up to the beautiful filly. Smaller than Thor, but not much smaller—good stature and fine-boned. Eric handed her a treat to give to the horse. "Hey, girl, you're certainly beautiful." She held the horse candy up to Solstice's muzzle, which she took and munched with pleasure.

Millicent turned, grinning, to Eric. "I think we're good!"

"Looks like it."

She climbed into the saddle, and everyone else mounted as well.

"Off we go!" Anthony broke into a trot, and the rest followed at either a casual walk or induced their mount to join Anthony and Thor.

Millicent stayed back with Clara and Eaton, becoming familiar with her mount. "How long has it been since you've been on horseback, Eaton?" she asked. "I don't think I've ever seen you ride, but you seem quite comfortable."

"I occasionally ride when no one else is. I like to ride at night. I come out and saddle up on occasion. But it's been close to two months since I've done that."

"Have you ridden Solstice?"

"No. She's only been here a couple weeks. But she's certainly fine."

"She is. A remarkably smooth gait—at least while walking. Let's see how she does at a trot." Millicent gently spurred the horse, who responded with little coaxing. Soon Solstice passed through the intended trot to a gentle run. It was glorious! Solstice quickly passed everyone but Thor. The beautiful horse was *fast!* She caught up to Thor and passed him, smooth as silk, and Millicent could tell the horse still had a lot of go-power in her. But she reigned her in and let Anthony catch up.

"What a sight to behold!" he exclaimed.

"She's remarkable. Is she racehorse stock?"

"Good intuition, Millicent. She is racehorse bred, but she has an issue with tendons. Because of that, I was able to buy her for, as saying has it, a song. A little more than a song, actually, but still, considerably less than her breeding value."

"*Oh, no!* Was it wrong for me to let her run?"

"I think it's okay once in a while, but, of course, she can't train, or run full tilt on a regular basis. She seemed to love it, though."

"She did. I hardly asked it of her."

"You'll have to come over and give her a bit of a workout on occasion."

"I'd love that."

Alison and Sage joined them. "That was some beautiful riding," Sage said.

"She's a great ride." Millicent leaned over and patted the horse. "She's remarkable, but, from what Anthony says, she needs to be handled gently."

"You're just the one for that," Alison said.

"Thank you, Alison. It would be lovely to ride her on occasion."

The four of them ambled on in companionable silence and eventually came to the copse of trees in the valley. The horses drank from the little stream running through the trees.

"Remember the fairies?" Alison and Sage said together. They broke into giggles.

"Oh yes, the fairies!" Anthony nodded. "That day we rode out here and Twinkle had that strong reaction. You said the fairies wanted her."

"But they couldn't have her," Alison nodded.

"I think they now would also want Solstice," Millicent observed. She looked over her shoulder, wondering where Eric and Michael were. They were trailing far behind. Even Clara and Eaton had ridden ahead of them. The two men ambled down the hillside, deep in conversation.

"Beautiful gait on Solstice," Eaton said when he and Clara joined them.

"True, true," everyone agreed.

The horses drank deeply of the fresh running water, even though it was barely above freezing.

"What's with Michael and Eric?" Anthony asked.

"Oh, they have something important to talk about," Sage said, giving Millicent a small glance.

Don't look at me, Millicent wanted to say. Was it possible that Eric would really tell Michael about her refusal to marry him? She turned Solstice around to directly watch Michael and Eric. Eric gestured toward where all the horses were. But Millicent knew he wasn't talking about all the horses. He was talking about one particular person.

Michael looked up at the group. They had come close enough that he made eye contact with Millicent. He gave her a look they'd shared many times at work, their "what's up with this?" look.

So! Eric had for sure told him her response to his proposal. She couldn't tell Michael in a return glance what was up. It would take pages to explain. And he'd just say something like "Are you crazy? Who wouldn't want to marry Eric?"

He'd be right. How could she explain to him it wasn't that she didn't want to marry Eric.

It was that she just could not imagine it.

The two men finally joined the group, and they all moseyed back to the horse barn, letting the horses have their rein. By the time they approached the horse barn, the group had fragmented again, and Millicent was alone. Michael came up alongside Solstice. "Okay, I'm going to be blunt because this is the only time we'll have alone. Why did you say no to my friend? Are you crazy?"

"Under the heading of 'none of your business,' I'll just say there's a lot more going on than I can share in the few yards from here to the horse barn. The short answer is, I can't quite imagine it."

"Do you *have* to imagine it?"

"So it would seem. But I'm unnerved that he would tell you. I would have hoped he considered it more private."

"I accidentally wrested it out of him. I teasingly asked him when you two were going to get hitched, and he surprised me by saying he'd asked yesterday, and you told him no. He really loves you, Millicent. Do you need more than that?"

"No, Michael, I don't. Maybe … maybe I need less."

They'd arrived at the horse barn. Millicent slid from Solstice and led her to her stall where she took off her saddle and blanket and bridle and brushed her down, wondering about her own comment. What did that mean, that she needed less than Eric loving her? That was ridiculous. And she didn't mean it. She wouldn't have Eric be any way other than exactly the way he was. Gorgeous, kind, sweet, blue eyes, and all.

Chapter 12

Christmas Eve Eve – Evening

Everyone went inside to stomp the chill out of their bones, to freshen up and to decide the next course of action.

When they reconvened in the kitchen, Clara put on a giant kettle for hot water and tea and made some coffee. From somewhere she materialized a giant plate of tomato and avocado sandwiches, and chickpea salad sandwiches.

"*Wow-oh-wow!*" Eric exclaimed "These chickpea salad sandwiches are incredible. You'll have to give me your recipe."

"Secret recipe," Clara laughed.

"When did you have time to make these sandwiches, Clara?" Alison asked. "You've been with us all day, and you made loaf after loaf of bread yesterday."

"I had my elf minions make them while we were out riding."

"I think she's telling the truth," Michael said. "But she knows we won't believe her, so her elven minions are safe. The question is, though, what do they expect in exchange for these delicious fairyland sandwiches?"

"They still cannot have Twinkle!" Alison insisted.

Everyone laughed while continuing to wonder how Clara managed to do all she did—and still have time to go horseback riding!

Suddenly Millicent leapt up. "Oh, no, I'm not taking care of my own responsibilities! Tina and John are coming over today with another mountain of fabulous food, and here I sit, stuffing my face. I've got to go!"

Eric stood. "I'll take you."

"I don't want to miss them!" Sage said standing. "I haven't seen Tina since the wedding."

"You stay and finish your lunch," Millicent said. If they come before you do, I'll try to keep them. Weeks ago I invited them to join us on Christmas Eve, so you'll see them tomorrow if, say, when I get to the front door I see a pile of food and no catering truck." Without even a good-bye, she stepped out the back door, hurried to Eric's truck and jumped in, with Eric close behind.

A few minutes later they were parked in front of Sage's mansion.

"No pile of food at the front door," Eric observed.

"No thank goodness. And it looks like no note either."

But just as Millicent unlocked the door, Tina and John's van came up the drive behind them.

"You must have heard them coming," Eric said.

"I guess! Cutting it close."

Tina jumped out of the van when it came to a stop

and hurried around to the side sliding doors. "Did you just get here?"

"We did! We went for a ride and were having a little light lunch when it hit me that you were coming sometime today. I should have pinned you down on the time."

"You could try. But that's always an approximation, at best. If something goes flat, or an oven breaks, or other some such catastrophe, we might be late. And if everything goes together perfectly, we'll be early."

John had gotten out of the van and was helping Tina bring the cart down the ramp. Millicent held the door open while they wheeled the cart inside. "As always, the kitchen is yours to do with as you please."

"Right. We gotta be on it. We have another job to do that has to be delivered tomorrow morning, and we want to be here when Michael and Sage come."

"That'll be a bit tricky unless you know how to travel back in time as they came yesterday. Sage wanted to return with us when I told her I had to rush back to be here for you, but I told her to enjoy her lunch. I said I'd try to keep you until she and Michael came. Do you think I can do that?"

"We'll see. Hopefully, they'll come before we've finished putting all these goodies away." Tina saw the loaves of bread. "Homemade bread! Who made it?"

"Clara, of course. You won't find me making bread as it's entirely arcane magic to me. In fact, the kitchen is pretty much a magician's lair in my mind."

Tina laughed heartily. "Thus assuring work for John and me."

"Oh, yes! Happily. I'm very pleased to exchange Sage's money for your wonderful talents. It's a win all around."

Tina and John secreted in various—arcane, as Millicent would say—places the new, and if possible, even more amazing, delicacies than the ones they'd brought the previous day. They finished and, as they loaded the cart back on the van, Michael and Sage drove into the driveway. Sage jumped out of the car and Tina leapt from the van. They hurried to one another, sharing a gigantic hug.

"I'm so glad I didn't miss you! After Millicent said she expected you today, I couldn't eat any more lunch. I nagged Michael to bring me over."

"Hardly nagging, darling when one says, 'would you pretty please take me home,' and bats those beautiful eyelashes at me, I'd likely take you anywhere you asked."

"But, Sage, here's my dilemma," Tina said. "John and I have a huge job that must be delivered tomorrow, and Millicent was kind enough to invite us to come tomorrow. So! We can either stay and chat this evening, but we won't be able to come tomorrow, because we'll be working all day. Or we go now and work all night, deliver the order in the morning, take a nap, get dressed in our Christmas finery and spend the rest of the day here with friends and family."

"Oh, yes, if I must choose, I want you here tomorrow, on Christmas Eve, when everyone is here, raving about your wonderful food. Off with you then, we'll see you tomorrow!"

Tina climbed back in the van. John turned around in the driveway, and everyone waved to everyone as they headed down the winding road.

"That was good enough," Sage said, as they went inside. Eric was in the kitchen, still working at putting away the last few new goodies.

"Sage and Michael came, just as Tina got in the van," Millicent told him, joining him in the kitchen.

"Great! Are Tina and John still coming tomorrow?"

"They are! They'll apparently pull one of their all-nighters tonight, deliver in the morning, take a nap, and come here later. So, that's two more people I'm sure of who will be here tomorrow."

"Are you really trying to count how many people will be here?"

"I guess so."

"And if you knew, at this late date, the exact number, what would you do differently?"

"I … ahhh, I guess nothing much different. But I would *know*. And there's comfort in knowledge."

"Think of it this way, sweetheart. This time tomorrow you'll have a very clear idea of how many people will be here, because most, if not all of them, will *be here*."

Millicent laughed. "Impeccable logic, dear. But that still doesn't inform me *tonight*."

"Oh! I forgot to bring in the gallon of mulled wine Clara sent with us," Michael called from the living room. "I'll bring it in."

At the same time, a faint, high-pitched barking could be heard from the back office. "And I'll go get Emdee."

Millicent went into the back office, greeted by her dancing little black dog. "You want to come and play with us?"

"Woof-woof-woof-woof!" Emdee insisted.

"All right then. But let's put on your little reindeer outfit, okay!"

"Woof!" Emdee agreed, following Millicent to the closet. She thrashed about and found a bag with *Love Your Pet Vet* printed across the side, and pulled out a brown sweater with a red and white collar, and white fluffy pompoms down the front, along with a pair of antlers she wasn't sure how they attached.

Emdee patiently let Millicent tug the sweater over her head and around her body. Then she put the antlers on Emdee's head. They were on a headband and a ribbon to tie under her chin. Pretty cute, if they stayed on! They returned to the living room, Emdee dancing like Prancer.

Oh, look, Michael, look at Emdee!" Sage cried. "She's prancing just like a reindeer. How does she know to do that?"

"I have no idea," Millicent answered. "She's never even seen this sweater nor these antlers. I just pulled it out of the sack and put it on her."

"She's amazing," Sage said, laughing at Emdee's adorable antics.

Michael, in the kitchen, pouring the mulled wine into a cauldron to simmer on the stove, looked over his shoulder to watch the little dog dance.

Eric came out of the pantry. "What's so entertaining?" Then he caught sight of the tiny reindeer and walked over to her. Stooping down to pet her he asked, "Are you the cleverest reindeer-dog in the world?"

"*Woof!*" Emdee agreed. "*Woof-woof!*"

Before long everyone had settled before the fireplace with mulled wine and a platter of cookies that Clara had sent along with the mulled wine. Michael and Eric built a beautiful roaring fire, and Millicent turned on some quiet Christmas music that joined with the crackling fire to make a cozy background of sound, accompanied by the aromas of mulled wine and Christmas tree.

Sage and Michael sat snuggled together on the sofa, Millicent had settled on a large pillow on the floor in front of the coffee table, while watching Michael and Eric build the perfect fire. Eric found another pillow and cuddled up next to Millicent on the floor.

The lavender shadows of winter evening gradually fell about the window and stole around the fireplace as the friends chatted about everything and nothing. The little dog, antlers somewhat askew, slept contentedly on Millicent's lap.

Though the moment could not be more perfect, Millicent couldn't keep her mind from going around and around on how many people were coming the next day, and longing to test, one last time, her snow machine.

"Who's coming of your relatives, Sage?" Eric asked.

Just like that! Millicent thought. Why hadn't she asked? It seemed verboten with the whole old-fashioned, no-one-knows-who's-coming-when, decree of Aunt Pelipa.

"Aunt Pelipa, and Uncle Halian, and my four cousins, as far as I know. And that's all I know. Don't ask me when they're coming, or if there'll be more or fewer. I'm in the dark with you."

Millicent put her head on Eric's shoulder, contented and—*finally!*—in the moment. Tomorrow would take care of itself. And Eric would help.

Chapter 13

Christmas Eve – Morning

Alison stretched in bed, reaching her arms to their fullest extent, then shrugging her shoulders. It was Christmas Eve, and she was back in her home. She felt delicious. The promises of the day filled her with child-like anticipation.

"It's Christmas Eve, my love," Anthony whispered, taking her outstretched hand and kissing her fingertips.

"It is! And I'm so happy. Christmas Eve, back at home. I'm … *so happy!*" She curled up in Anthony's embrace, warm, and safe, and cuddly.

"Happy is not a big enough word for me," Anthony held her even closer. "Nor is delighted, contented, elated, blissful, or over-the-moon. *I'm rapturous!* And awed that you are here again with me. That you're back in my life is the greatest miracle of the last year, and I'm profoundly grateful."

Alison sighed a deep tranquil sigh. "I agree, my darling. All is well." She tried to escape his embrace. "But we must not linger anymore! There's much to be done today, time to get up! I hear Clara down in the kitchen—she's probably been at it for hours, and Eaton seems to be banging around doing who-knows-what, and it's …" she glanced at the clock, "*already nine o'clock!* Who do we think we are, lazing about while others slave?!"

"We're the Lord and Lady of the castle, and we may do as we please," Anthony replied, nuzzling the nape of her neck.

"Well, dear Lord of the castle, the Lady pleases to get herself up, gathered, presentable, and ready to travel to the neighboring castle."

"But," Anthony said, a nervous note in his voice, "I need to say … that is … I'm *going* to say that if I'm on the phone today rather much …."

"Today? It's Christmas Eve, Anthony, no business today!"

"I understand and agree with your sentiment. But I have … I'm working on a Christmas gift and it requires a bit of clandestine-seeming phone conversations. Please don't take it badly."

"You have something you can't tell even me?"

"That is the nature of surprise."

"Goodness, I don't know how you're going to make something come together at this last minute."

"Well, I've been working on it for … awhile."

"All right. I'll ignore your 'clandestine-seeming' private phone conversations today." She escaped his embrace and went to her closet, peeking out at him. A very pleased-with-himself grin grew on his face as he put his hands behind his head.

After a few moments, she came out of the closet holding up two breathtaking floor-length gowns, one a brilliant Christmas red, the other an elegant, deep royal blue. "Opinion? I can't decide which to wear. The red is, of course, Christmas all the way. But everyone is likely to be in red. The blue is pure Victorian styling, and fulfills the 'old-fashioned' theme ... I don't know, I just can't deci...."

Anthony began to sing in his beautiful baritone ... *"She wore blue velvet, bluer than velvet were her eyes, warmer than May her tender sighs, love was ours ...."*

"Oh! Anthony!" Alison dropped the gowns onto the oriental carpet and rushed into his arms. "Blue velvet it is. The day can wait."

* *

Before the crack of dawn, Millicent was up, tiptoeing about, hoping not to disturb anyone—including Emdee, who would certainly bark with joy, as was her habit in the morning.

She slipped into some scruffy sweats, then went down into the back office where she kept more or less hidden her rough-and-tumble outdoor clothing. She pulled on her forest camouflage zippered hoodie, her well-worn all-terrain boots, her extra-warm gloves, and slipped outside, thrashing her way through the foliage—not too thick in the winter—around the mansion to where the snow machine sat upon its scaffolding. She was surprised to see that the machine's scaffolding was above the second-floor windows—an unanticipated bonus! Snow for anyone who stayed in the bedrooms at this end of the second floor.

She shifted around in her mind who would stay where. She'd put Aunt Pelipa and Uncle Halian, honored elders, in these rooms.

She'd be inclined to do a happy dance right there in the fallen leaves if only the machine would work. She recalled that the boss of the three stooges had said that one of them had forgotten to push the 'on' button. An 'on' button was obviously not on the ground level scaffolding. Stepping back, she saw what looked like it might be an 'on' button on the machine, where it sat above the second-floor window. If absolutely necessary—that was, if it refused to work—she could perhaps reach it.

If absolutely necessary. She hurried back around the mansion and into her office. Still, no one was up! Divesting herself of her gloves, boots, and hoodie, she hurried into the living room, grabbed up the snow machine remote and pressed the "gentle snow" button. Waiting.

Waiting.

And then … gentle snow! *Beautiful, gentle snow!* What a relief. She quickly shut it off and right then heard Sage and Michael stirring about. She put the remote on the mantle, then scurried upstairs to get into something a bit more presentable than her work sweats.

After changing, she relaxed for "just a moment" in bed with Emdee and, *somehow*, fell back asleep. Clattering in the kitchen woke her with a start. *9:30!* She leapt up,

Emdee barking happily. She ran downstairs, her little black dog at her heels.

"*Ah!*" Michael teased, "Her highness awakens!"

Millicent kept her early morning foraging around the exterior of the mansion to herself, and grinned, taking the ribbing.

"Leave her alone," Sage said from the living room, stretched out on the sofa in her green silk dressing gown. "She's off the clock, and may do as she pleases."

I'm hardly off the clock, Millicent thought. But that doesn't need to be mentioned, either.

"I doubt Millicent considers herself off the clock—this day, of all days," Eric defended, coming out of the pantry. "She's been preparing for today for weeks."

Millicent was happy to see that he'd finished his morning routine of caring for Anthony's horses. Christmas Eve breakfast together! Made by himself and Michael, with her darling Emdee dancing around everyone and everything, spreading joy.

It was a dream she could not have even imagined the previous Christmas. And it was real.

"I stand corrected," Sage agreed with Eric. "She's not likely to consider today a holiday. But do come over here now, dear Millicent, and sit with me. Let's pretend, for a few minutes at least, that there's not one single thing you need concern yourself with."

"All right. I'll try." Millicent joined Sage on the sofa, sitting sideways so she could watch the two beautiful men make tea and coffee and whatever else they were engaged in. "As there's to be so many yummy treats all day long, I believe I'll just have some fruit and a cup of tea."

"Coming right up!" Eric brought a tray of sliced bananas, oranges, apples, and pineapple arranged beautifully around a mountain of big, fat, red Holiday grapes, which he placed in the middle of the coffee table, while Michael brought a tray of cups, a pot of hot water, a variety of teas, a pot of coffee, and honey.

"Couldn't be more perfect," Millicent curled up in the corner of the sofa to make room for Michael and Eric.

"Perfectly cozy," Eric said, picking up a small plate. "Don't move, Millicent. Tell me what you fancy, and I'll put it on this charming little Christmas plate I found in the pantry. I discovered an entire set of Christmas holly china, in a box in the pantry, dug it out, and I'm in the process of washing it all by hand. I don't want to put it in the dishwasher."

"*Really!*" Sage and Millicent exclaimed together. They exchanged a glance and broke into giggles.

"Neither of us had any idea there was a set of Christmas china. How many place settings?" Millicent explained.

"A dozen."

"Not quite enough."

"But more than before," Eric said. "Glass half-full!"

"Yes, my dear," Millicent agreed. "And more festive than if there were none. Glass full and over-flowing!"

"Full and over-flowing," all three of her friends intoned together.

Millicent stood and went to the mantle to light the candles. "It's maybe a bit early for candles, but they add to the mood." The swaying flame in the fat red candles cast a dancing light on the shadows of the mantle.

"Do you want me to make a fire?" Eric asked.

"Not just yet. Save your fire starter skills for later." She studied Michael and Sage for a moment, the two of them communing in silence. So together. So of one mind.

So mystical. Could she possibly have anything even remotely like that with Eric? It seemed unlikely if she wasn't even aware that he had intended to ask her to marry him.

Marry Eric.

The thought made her feel flushed and a bit dizzy. It suddenly hit her hard.

It became ... *real.*

"Are you all right?" Eric asked, alarmed. He started to stand.

"Yes, yes. I'm fine. Don't get up. Just a bit of vertigo. All the aromas—which I love—are perhaps a bit much for me. The candles are scented. I'll just ... move away." She went to the window on the far side of the fireplace, knowing they all watched her closely. With her back to them she said, "Stop looking at me."

They laughed uneasily. "Guilty," Sage said. "But we're just, you know, concerned. You've been working so hard, and if you're not feeling well ... we love you, that's all."

"I'm fine." She forced a smile on her face and turned to them. "Really. Just a moment of vertigo, and it's gone.

"Ahm, now, to change the subject and get it off me—I'd love to hear about your life. We email all the time, but that's superficial and generally about business. I want to know more about your common day-to-day bits."

"Me too," Eric agreed. "Tell us about your real, everyday life."

Millicent returned to the sofa and Eric cuddled her. Calming, even if her heart still jumped about in a funny way, and her mind seemed to have gone to Alpha Centauri.

"We have a modest house," Sage began. "It's a bit away from the heart of the reservation. Of course, by the standards of most everyone there, our house is big and elegant. We hold a lot of community events in our home, so it needs to be somewhat spacious."

"I work to find decent jobs for people, and make sure they're getting paid a good wage," Michael added.

"And I work with mothers and their children," Sage said. "I teach them the basics of childcare and healthcare, and make sure they have the healthcare they need. I generally end up driving people to the hospital, which is some distance, once or twice a week.

"And in return," Michael continued, "we are blessed with love and spiritual togetherness, and community. Warmth, tribal unity, kindness, homely, sweet gifts …."

"Yes," Sage agreed. They were both silent for a few reflective moments. "It's not all roses and sunshine," Sage noted. "There are problems. Issues with prejudice, issues with government, issues with some of the people who have deep magical beliefs, which I cannot deny, I've seen too much that outsiders would call paranormal. But, it can pose problems, when hard times are blamed on an individual."

"And so it is everywhere," Eric intoned softly.

"True," Sage agreed. "True and too true. But, overall, Michael and I feel that we receive much more than we give."

"Amen, my darling. It's impossible to explain. Especially sitting in the midst of this," he waved his hand around. "So much plenty, so many things."

"Oh!" Millicent said with insight. "Do you want to get rid of the 'things?'"

"We talk about it," Sage nodded. "But no, not as it stands at present. Though this is quite a lot of house, it's set up, and essentially cares for itself. And then you, dear Millicent, live here and care for it and, well, all my business. You know, of course, that we give most of the money generated from Aunt Victoria's monies and businesses to Native American issues, as you're the one who tends to it!"

"But … I don't need to live in this mansion!" Millicent protested. "If you want to liquidate it …."

"No, I'm not quite ready to do that. It *is* the family estate, and next door to Michael's family, so, as it's essentially self-supporting, it's nice to have, where everyone can come. Like right now, on Christmas Eve, for example!" Sage smiled warmly at Millicent. "I would have some very different feelings about it, if not for you, Millicent. Your head for business simply amazes me. How you make money grow is mystifying and wonderful.

"We thank you. And the whole tribe thanks you."

"Oh, you embarrass me," Millicent said. So much emotional input and the day was still young! "But please, don't ask me to even boil a pot of water!"

"Of course not," Eric. said. "That's what I'm here for." He kissed her on her forehead.

"Yes," she agreed. "Water boiling, tea-steeping, fruit-cutting, Christmas-dishes-finding. All skills I've never mastered."

Chapter 14

Christmas Eve – Afternoon

The day slid into afternoon with everyone nibbling at the goodies that were for later, in the midst of cheerful chatting.

In the early afternoon, Eric got a call from Anthony. "Strange!" he said after disconnecting. "He says he needs me to come over directly, but he's entirely cryptic about why. Off I go, then. I'll be back … well, I don't know when. But, hopefully before too long."

"Oh!" Millicent said, curious and a bit sad to have him leave their comradely gathering. "I'm sure it's important, but hurry back."

"I will … I think." He stepped out the front door and they soon heard his truck driving down the hill.

"I wonder what that's about?" Michael frowned.

"One would think he'd recruit you before Eric," Sage said.

"It probably has something to do with the horses," Millicent observed. "I hope nothing's wrong."

"Yes, indeed. If anything *is* wrong with any of the horses, we likely won't see Uncle Anthony today at all." Michael frowned.

"And Eric, as well." Millicent was not happy with the thought of *this* possible outcome.

"It's probably just something about the place that Eric is familiar with, and Michael isn't since he doesn't live here anymore," Sage said hopefully.

"Whatever it is," Millicent added brightly, "The show must go on. I think, if you don't mind, I'll go upstairs and get dressed for the evening. As we still don't know when anyone's coming, I'd rather be ready. And I have a darling little Victorian outfit for Emdee if she likes it."

"That's a perfect idea. Both Michael and I have primping to do, too, as we're wearing Victorian outfits, which have stays and buttons and what all that demand a lot of attention."

Millicent chuckled. "That was exactly my thought, and why it seems like a good idea to take time to put it all together."

The three of them made their way upstairs, Emdee racing ahead. "Last one downstairs is a Christmas elf," Millicent teased.

"*Ohhh!*" Sage cried. "I *want* to be the Christmas elf! Don't look for me until, as they say, you see the whites of my eyes."

* *

Millicent went into her room and looked at the dress she'd stressed and struggled over actually purchasing, although she'd fallen in love with it on sight. She thought it beautiful but perhaps too flamboyant, then decided not to get it. After coming home, she could not forget it. She decided to go back and get it, fully realizing it was likely to be gone. Much to her surprise, the gorgeous Victorian-styled dress was still there, and so, feeling entirely out of character, she bought it.

It now hung on the edge of the open closet door. Beautiful, simply hanging there like an art object. But still more "ostentatious" in her mind than anything she'd ever worn. *However!* It fulfilled her notion of Aunt Pelipa's decree to have an "old-fashioned" Christmas.

She turned from the dress and left her room, going down the hall to one of the rooms that overlooked Anthony's place. She remembered how, ever so long ago it now seemed, she'd moved out this room for the very reason that it overlooked not only Anthony's place but faced Michael's room. When Michael declared his love for Sage, she didn't want to see his room, occupied or not, and had moved down the hall.

Now she wanted to see Anthony's place because that's where, at this moment, Eric was. As she looked, she was very surprised to see the limo pull out of the garage and move down the driveway. She couldn't see who was in the car. Was it possible that they were coming over this early? She'd better get a hustle on if that was the case. She waited for a few seconds to see the limo turn into Sage's driveway.

But it did not! It continued on down the country road. She dashed to the next room, and out that window saw the limo disappear over the hill.

What was up? *So strange!* Where would anyone be going now? Maybe Clara urgently needed something for her baking. But no, they'd have it delivered. Wait, it was Christmas Eve. Maybe they couldn't get a delivery today. But, wait again. They'd never take the *limo* just to pick up something.

This was a strange mystery. One which she could not solve standing here at the window. She must do what must be done, regardless of what was going on next door. "Abandon all musings regarding things you know nothing about," she told herself aloud and returned to her room. Looking at her dress again, she felt even more disheartened imagining herself in it.

Emdee had quietly padded around after her, into one bedroom, into the next and back to her own room. She looked up at her as if asking, "What's bothering you?"

"*I'm* bothering me!" Millicent said. "But we can't do much about that, can we?"

"*Woof!*" Emdee said. It was a soft and gentle "woof," making Millicent laugh. As if her little friend knew exactly what she'd asked, and offered reassurance.

"Well, if you say so," she said, patting the little dog on her head. "Shall we dress you first in your beautiful little Victorian outfit?"

"*Woof! Woof!*" Emdee answered, hopping and leaping about from the undivided attention. Millicent got out the little outfit that she'd found in *Love Your Pet Vet*—she could not believe her eyes when she saw the darling doggie hat and cape of almost the very same red and green plaid as her dress.

She sat down on the floor and fussed with putting the Victorian cape on Emdee, a barely visible strap wrapped around each of her front legs to keep it in place, along with a beautiful wide, shiny red satin ribbon, which she tied loosely around Emdee's neck.

"Next we'll put on this too-cute-for-words matching little cap, okay?"

"*Arrr-woof!*" Emdee agreed, standing patiently while Millicent placed the hat over two little holes for her ears, then tying another bright red satin ribbon into a big bow, off to the side. "Are you all right with that, my pet?"

"*Woof-woof-woof!*" Emdee pranced about the bedroom, knowing she looked adorable.

Millicent burst into laughter. "You are *soooo* funny, you adorable little dog. I wish I had your confidence and could prance around like that, once I get into this beautiful contraption."

Resignedly, she began to put on all the components of her outfit, considerably more complicated than Emdee's, making it very clear why women in Victorian times had a "lady's maid."

Half an hour later, she cautiously allowed herself to take a serious look at the effect, ready to jettison the whole thing and slip into something a bit more like her—more "quiet."

She gasped. *It was not awful at all!* She looked like this was the very dress she had always meant to wear on Christmas Eve.

The beautiful red and green plaid rustle-y satin of the empire waistline fell to the floor, billowing slightly with the bell-shaped skirt. Gold threads ran through the plaid, catching the light prettily. The low-cut red velvet bodice had long sleeves almost to her fingertips. Was the bodice too much? No, she decided. Just enough. Though she was a tiny little thing, the dress accentuated her delicate feminine form.

And it was good.

Would Eric like it? She felt certain that the answer to that question would be a resounding "*yes!*"

She'd found a pair of red Victorian hair combs, actual antiques, made of "paste" as they called it, in a little antique shop. She wasn't sure what "paste" meant, as the stones were very sparkly and not like any paste she was familiar with. She'd played around with the combs a bit when she got them but had never gotten serious about what she might do with her baby-soft hair, generally difficult to arrange by anything other than just brushing.

She decided to forego the notion of putting her hair up in any way. It would just fall down and preoccupy her. She pulled her hair back from her temples and placed the two combs symmetrically on either side of the crown of her head.

Studying the effect she saw it, too, was good, accentuating her high cheekbones.

She applied a bit of golden sparkly eye shadow, mascara, lipstick, and just a hint of sparkly pink on the crest of her cheekbones.

And in her mind, she declared it was altogether good!

In fact, she'd almost completely forgotten about the mystery of the limo heading down Anthony's drive.

Almost. But not quite.

She turned to Emdee, who had finally gotten bored of watching her preen, something she rarely did, and asked, "What do you think, Miss Emdee? Am I acceptable?"

"*Woof!*" Emdee exclaimed, jumping up and then off the bed, dancing around Millicent sitting at her dresser. "*Woof, woof, woof-woof-woof!*" she further declared.

"Well, I guess it's good, then." she bent over to put on her strappy three-inch red heels. "Unless everyone else wears three-inch heels, I, for once, won't be the little shrimp! Let's go downstairs."

Millicent cautiously navigated the stairs. Neither three-inch heels nor floor-length dresses were items she wore, and both together seemed like a recipe for disaster.

"I'm going downstairs. I'm not the elf!" she called back up toward Sage and Michael's room.

"We're right behind you," Michael called.

"*Almost*," Sage added.

Just as Millicent reached the bottom stair, the door chimes rang. She opened the door to Tina and John.

And there was the elf! Tina wore an elven costume, with a red pointy hat, bells on the tip, red shoes with green trim, and great big, over-arching curly points with bells on the ends. As she came in, she jingled and jangled. She wore green tights, and a short red velvet dress—*very short*—with a no-holds-barred plunging neckline, and a wide black shiny belt with a gigantic gold buckle. Chubby and voluptuous.

"*Ahem!*" Millicent exclaimed, contemplating Tina's décolletage, while trying to ignore it.

"You're just jealous," Tina smirked.

"Probably," Millicent answered. "Well, come in. Where's John?"

"He's bringing yet more goodies."

He popped through the door as Millicent was closing it, from head to foot looking like a gnome. He wore a stand up pointy red hat, no bells, a ragged-edged green tunic, brown pants that just passed his knees, also raggedy, and big, bulbous red shoes.

"*Ho-ho-ho!*" he said, looking Millicent up and down. "*Merrry* Christmas! I didn't know you had that flare in you! Well done. Quite the beauty."

"Turn it off," Tina said.

"She doesn't hold a candle to you, my fluffy delight. As you well know." He stumbled in his clumsy shoes into the kitchen and, finding a tray, arranged the last-minute goodies.

As Tina and Millicent joined him, Sage and Michael came down the stairs. Sage wore a floor-length, flowing green velvet gown with a tall, dramatic, Queen Anne collar, and finger-tip sleeves that came to a point. Her amazing waist-length natural platinum blond hair, which she'd worn in a braid over her shoulder since she came, she'd now released, and it cascaded down her back in gorgeous waves. She wore a four-strand pearl necklace with matching earrings of four graduated pearls.

"*Lord save me*," John whispered, as Sage, all mystically beautiful, six-foot-plus of her, appeared to float down the stairs.

Tina jabbed him with her elbow. But there was no one who would disagree that this was a sight one would never forget. Millicent finally took in Michael, two steps behind Sage, in a dark Victorian frock coat, slim-fitting and falling to his knees, under which he wore a bright red waistcoat with a matching red bow tie, and dark, Victorian trousers, looking as if he just stepped out of a Victorian clothing catalog.

Sage and Michael came up to them in the kitchen area, smiling.

"What are you all gawking at?" Sage asked, towering over everyone but Michael.

"What the hel … heck do you think? *YOU*, of course. *Have you seen you?*" John blurted.

Sage laughed while taking in Tina's outfit. "I see I'm not the elf," she said, giving her friend a big hug. "You look so adorable. And sexy."

"I thought so too until I saw you and Millicent."

Sage finally focused on Millicent. "Oh—you're gorgeous! Look at her, Michael."

"I'm looking," Michael said, giving Millicent a wink. "You're finally acknowledging your beauty."

"I don't know. It wasn't easy getting into this dress for real instead of just playing dress-up in the clothing store. It's not too much?"

"Not too much. Not too little," Michael said.

"Just right," Sage agreed. "So … what can we do?"

"Nothing," Millicent answered. "We'll start to put some of the finger food items on the dining room table and the coffee table. The mulled wine needs to be warmed. And, whatever else." Millicent couldn't keep the thought of the limo going down the road out of her mind. What if it was Eric in the limo, and he was off to do something that kept him from being here for the entire day?

"Michael, I saw Anthony's limo pull out of the garage shortly after we went upstairs. What do you think of that?"

He and Sage had moved to the living room, but he came back to Millicent. "*Whoa!* You're tall!"

"Three-inch heels."

"I see. Well, yes, that seems strange. Maybe they needed something, and since it's Christmas Eve, they couldn't get it delivered."

"My thought exactly. But in the limo? I'm hoping it wasn't Eric sent on a mission that will keep him from being with us much longer."

"Me too!" Michael joined them in getting out the comestibles.

"I feel like a garden slug, sitting here while you all labor away," Sage called.

"Not to worry, my dear, enjoy your little slug break. You've earned it."

She jumped up. "I know what I'll do, I'll light all these candles that are everywhere. Don't forget them later."

"Thank you, Sage," Millicent said. "That really is a big help. I wanted them lighted, but had planned on asking Eric to do it while I attended to—well, the stuff I'm attending to!"

They all ran about setting things up, lighting candles, turning on music, completely in a jovial mood, while, at the same time, everyone waited for others to appear.

Suddenly they were all in the kitchen again, grinning with anticipation.

"*The moment arrives*," John said in serious, hushed, gnome tones.

"Well, I just wish …." Millicent said.

The front door chimes rang and Michael went to answer their call.

"…. Eric was here."

Michael opened the door, and in stepped Eric, in a turn of the 20th-century cowboy outfit, red buttons on his red plaid shirt, and a big cowboy hat, which he removed and held in his hands after he stepped through the door.

"Why didn't you say that an hour ago, Millicent?" Tina asked.

"I would have, if I'd know I had that sort of magic."

Eric looked around as if he was looking for something. Millicent came out of the kitchen and moved toward him. As he took in that this glorious sight was what he'd been looking for, he dropped his hat.

Everyone laughed.

"Yeah. She's a hat dropper," John said.

"Stuff it," Tina teased.

"Millicent," he whispered.

"Yes?"

"I mean, *Millicent!*" He took a deep breath. I … you …."

"We, them," John added. "What's with this guy? Pick up your hat and give her a kiss."

"Pick up your hat, my dear," Millicent agreed, "but let's save the kiss for later."

Eric picked up his hat.

"By the way, cowboy," she added, "you're not so bad yourself."

"Where are Anthony and Alison and Clara and Eaton?" Michael asked.

"Anthony and Alison are right behind me. Clara gave Anthony a big box to bring that appears pretty heavy. Clara and Eaton are working on a last-minute project."

Anthony came through the door struggling under the weight of the box he carried. He was dressed similarly to Michael, except his frock coat covered a pair of festive grey and white striped trousers. His waistcoat matched the grey of his trousers, topped with a Christmas green bowtie.

"*Merry Christmas, Merry Christmas,*" he cried. "Let me through! I have to put this down before I drop it."

Everyone parted and let him through, then followed him into the kitchen, curious as to what he had that was so heavy. He opened the box. In it was a set of Christmas china.

"It looks just like what I discovered in the pantry!" Eric exclaimed.

"Good observation," Anthony grinned. "Clara said that many years ago she noted this Christmas pattern here in this house. How, I don't know, I don't remember Victoria and her husband ever having a Christmas party.

But, anyway, Clara thought it would be appropriate to buy the same pattern, in case our two households ever decided to have a shared Christmas."

"She's prescient!" Sage exclaimed.

"She *does* seem to have that quality," Anthony agreed. "She spent a couple hours washing it by hand today, so it's ready to be set out."

The chimes rang again.

Anthony looked around. *"Oh, no! Alison!"* He hurried to the door and opened it, extending his hand, Alison took it and stepped inside. "Sorry, darling!"

"My shoe caught in my hem," she said. Then looked around at everyone staring at her.

"Exquisite, Aunt Alison," Michael finally said.

"That's exactly what I said," Anthony concurred.

"Merrrrrrry Christmas!" John said, taking in Alison's beauty, then wolf-whistled. "This is surely a gnome's favorite home!"

"I don't know what's gotten into you," Tina said.

"I'm a gnome. You said you wanted me to be a gnome. Gnomes are dirty old men, except they're not men. But I think they're generally pretty dirty, and they are certainly old."

"All right, already!" Tina put her hand over his mouth and he made loud kissing noises against it.

"Queens and elves and gnomes, oh my!" Michael laughed. "Quite the Christmas Eve."

"And more to come," Sage agreed. "As soon as Aunt Pelipa and company arrive."

"And more to come," Michael nodded.

Chapter 15

Christmas Eve – Evening

Although there was a growing sense of anticipation waiting for the rest of the company to arrive, there was already a happy Christmas Eve mood in everyone. Exclamations were made over the tree. Anthony and Michael went out to the car to bring yet more giant armloads of gifts and placed them under—or near—the tree. Eric suddenly had a couple of armloads of brightly wrapped packages he slipped under the tree. Millicent just barely noticed him do it, he was so subtle.

Tina and John seemed to be sort of bickering in the kitchen, but when Millicent went into the kitchen to see if she could temper what was going on, she stepped into the midst of them giving one another a sweet kiss, and she realized that they were just playing their roles to the hilt. She a mischievous elf, he a grouchy gnome.

It was pretty cute and added fun to the festivities. Millicent grinned. "Okay you two, you're off the clock! We can feed ourselves with the amazing, *amazing* yummy edibles you've brought. Time to take a load off your underworld, otherworld feet and join the party! Come on now, into the living room with you."

"If you insist," Tina said.

"I do. And Sage no doubt would prefer you in there with her."

"*I would!*" Sage called, overhearing Millicent.

The three of them went into the living room. Sage gestured for Tina and John to sit by her, while everyone watched as Eric lit the fire that he'd laid out earlier.

Millicent glanced at the mantle to assure the snow machine remote was where it ought to be. She turned down the room lights, letting the candles and firelight take over. Everyone glowed with a nearly phantasmic beauty. Christmas music tranquilly suffused the air, the aroma of the Christmas tree, mulled wine, and edible delicacies mingled with the scent of burning wood.

The moment was filled to overfull with *something*.

Anthony and Alison, sitting in the wing-backed chairs on either side of the fireplace, in front of the windows, exchanged a look.

Michael happened to be standing by Millicent. As if she'd whispered her thoughts out loud he said, "It's just like the snow globe shows. *Love*. That's what this moment is about—love, and nothing else.

"Sage is the other part of me, as you have told me yourself," he continued. "But I will always love you, my precious little friend. You gave me joy and silliness and happiness during the darkest time of my life. I was so depressed at that awful job. Even though I don't think I knew it consciously, I knew my day would be saved by the tiny woman who brought my mail—even on days when I didn't have mail."

"*Oh, Michael!*" Words she had so longed to hear—well, perhaps without that part about Sage—at that time when, unknown by him, she, too, was profoundly depressed. Needing to support her three siblings. Desperately, or so she thought, desperately in love with Michael, who always laughed at her jokes.

Now, everything was different. *Everything was wonderful.* She was happy and even relieved that Michael and Sage had found one another. Because that path let her discover her own true love. Instead of pining for someone who would never love her in that way, she was loved by Eric. Sweetly and completely.

She looked over at him. He stood by Sage, mulled wine in hand, chatting with her. As if her look was spoken words, he glanced at her, a wide grin crossing his features. He gestured toward her with his wine glass, saying something to Sage. She looked over at Millicent and nodded, smiling.

They were saying how beautiful she looked. They were saying how much they cared for her, how happy they were for her. She grinned back at them, and the flush she felt was not just from the fire.

Suddenly, something was happening in the room. Everyone's near lethargy in the warmth and food was brought to attention.

John had gotten up from the sofa. He stood and scrabbled around with the pocket of his short, brown, gnome pants. He pulled out something small.

The room fell to a hush, with even a break in the music. The grandfather clock ticked.

"Tina, my darling," he said, taking off his silly gnome hat, and getting down on one knee. "I love you more than life itself. It's Christmas Eve, it's all about love. Nothing makes sense to me when you're not around." He reached up and took her hand. "You are the most beautiful woman in the world in so many ways. I never had a clue about love, until I met you. Love of my life, will you marry me?"

There was a sigh from everyone, too touched by the scene to move a muscle, expecting to hear but one word, followed by emotion and cheers.

Tina spoke one word, followed by emotion, but it took everyone by surprise.

"No!" she cried, jumping up. "No!" she cried again, and ran from the living room into the pantry and slammed the door—not easily done with a folding door.

Shocked, John didn't move—on one knee, his hand reaching out to an empty space on the sofa.

Sage stood and moved across the living room, the dining room, through the kitchen and to the pantry. "Tina," she said.

Tina said nothing.

"Tina," Sage said again.

The pantry door opened a crack. Sage stepped through it and closed the door again.

Millicent knew that everyone, along with herself, had a mental picture of the chubby elf and the Amazonian beauty in the tiny space they were now standing in.

The louvered door provided no sound barrier to the conversation.

"My friend," Sage said, "what is going on? Don't you love John? I've only seen you dote on him from the very first time you met him."

"*Really?*" John whispered, still not moving.

"I love him. Silly question, Sage."

"Not really, under the circumstances."

Silence.

"Oh, yes. I see your point."

"So, why did you say 'no'?"

"Because … because everything is perfect the way it is. I don't want to rock the boat.…"

Millicent exchanged a glance with Eric, then looked down at the oriental carpet, stunned to hear her own words.

"You will not rock the boat. He loves you. Love wants to share itself. When two people love each other, and everyone around them loves them, then a testament to that love, in other words, marriage, can only nurture love, and make it grow. You're not just saying yes to John, you're saying yes to an energy that builds strength, compassion, joy, and happiness when that love is true.

"And the love between you and John is true and beautiful."

"But why did he have to do it when we're in these silly costumes? *Why?* It's so, I don't know. It's not romantic. I look silly."

"You may not say that about my friend," Sage said. "The two of you have brought levity and joy to our Christmas Eve. You know how to not take things too seriously. You know how to bring the outdoors in, to bring legend and beliefs into your celebrations of Christmas, the season of love.

"You're not silly. You're mystical! Christmas is a time when maybe, just maybe we allow ourselves to accept a bit of mystical belief. A child born of love.

"You don't have to say yes to John. But he's out there on one knee, or at least he was, his heart open, and not ashamed or shy to declare to anyone and everyone his love for you, and his desire to make a life-long commitment to that love. It's none of my business if you must say no, but I believe, if you are true to yourself, you would say yes. Am I wrong?"

"I'm confused," Tina said.

Everyone chuckled.

Alison exchanged a look with Anthony, and her eyes said, "yes."

"If you love him and share his ideal of spending a life together, would you say yes to him?"

"I … I suppose, yes."

John jumped up and ran to the pantry, tripping over his big, floppy shoes. Righting himself, he knocked on the pantry door.

"Now who?" Tina asked.

"Me, Tina. It's me."

Sage opened the door and stepped out. John stepped in and, again got down on one knee. There was no room to close the door.

"My darling Tina, I love you more than life itself … I …."

"Oh for pity's sake! Yes, already!"

John opened the little box, took out the ring and put it on Tina's finger. Everyone watched as she held it up to her eyes. "*OMG*, John, how did you afford a rock like this? Is it real?"

Everyone laughed.

"It's real my chubby baby. You know me, nothing but real, all the way." He stood and kissed her. Tina reached out and closed the pantry door again.

Sage returned to Michael, fairly floating across the rooms, looking beatific. Michael put his arm around her.

"*Finally!*" Sage said.

Those who knew that Tina had, before John, a history of horrible men, knew what Sage meant about her beloved, oldest friend.

Millicent had moved to Eric. "I believe—*yes!*"

Eric said nothing, but he held her close and closer.

Chapter 16

Christmas Eve – More Company

Finally, Tina and John emerged from the pantry, looking a bit disheveled, but glowing.

"Look, everybody," Tina crowed, flashing her engagement ring. "I'm getting married!"

"We know," several people replied.

"Look at this ring!" Tina said to Millicent.

"It's beautiful!" Millicent exclaimed. She was herself a bit surprised at the size of it. Did they really make that much money with their catering? Or would John be paying for it forever?

It didn't matter. What mattered was they loved one another. They were such a perfect match. Anyone could see it. Were she and Eric a perfect match? Did other people see them as a perfect match, as clearly as she saw that Tina and John belonged together? She had told Eric yes, but she still wondered what he saw in her, why he loved her. She knew she loved him enough for both of them.

Even while she had these thoughts, she also had to acknowledge that he loved her as she would never be loved by anyone else. They belonged together. Plain and simple. Part of the package deal was Millicent's self-doubt and poor self-esteem. Eric seemed to her perfect. She'd have to figure out something less than perfect about him so they'd be more of a match. She grinned to herself.

"What's that secret grin?" Eric asked.

"You caught me. I was just thinking that I had to discover something less than perfect about you."

"There's plenty."

"I don't see it."

There's …."

"Wait! What's that?" Millicent asked.

"Why, it sounds like carolers," Eric said.

"How could carolers even find their way up here, in the dark?"

"Let's go see them. Maybe they want some cookies."

As they moved to the front door, everyone joined them. Millicent opened the door and was greeted with a large group that she could not exactly see who all it was. She recognized Aunt Pelipa and Uncle Halian at the front of the group. They were dressed in beautiful traditional Zuni attire. Then she saw Sage's four young cousins, all dressed in Dickens' outfits. Clara and Eaton were on either side of the young people, dressed in Edwardian garb.

But there were more people, in the darkness, that she could not make out. There was one beautiful voice that was so very much like a voice she knew. She stepped out into the chilled evening, and everyone else stepped out with her. The carolers sang on. Curious, frowning, she moved to the back of the group. There were two couples, she could not make out who they were.

Michael, who had stepped out beside Eric and Millicent, called out, "Mom! Dad!"

David and Marsha, Michael's parents, whom Millicent had met once, years before, stopped singing and embraced their son.

Then, much to her surprise, Eric, sounding shocked, exclaimed, "*Dad! Mom!*" Eric's parents moved from the group to hug Eric.

Three young people continued singing on.

"*Oh! Oh! Oh!*" Millicent could say nothing more as her three precious and beautiful siblings, flew into her arms. "*Oh! My babies!*" she cried, hugging them all to her. "How did you get here?"

"Anthony bought us plane tickets," Stephanie said.

"And Eric came and got us from the airport," Baby added.

"In the limo?"

"In a really big, long car, yeah," Peter said, excited. "He picked us up and took us to Anthony's giant home, and everyone came, and then Eaton drove us halfway up the driveway, and we sang Christmas carols to the door."

"These people are so wonderful," Stephanie added. "Do you know, they are real Zuni Indians?"

"I know, Stephie. They're Sage's relatives."

"And we met Michael's parents, and Eric's parents. And Eaton and Clara organized everything after Anthony set it all up," Baby chirped excitedly. "Are you surprised?"

"More than surprised. Oh my goodness, so much more than surprised."

While everyone else gradually made their way inside, Millicent and Eric stayed outside with their families, in the gentle light of the candy canes and the children on horses.

"These are Millicent's siblings I told you about, Mom and Dad," Eric said, "that she took care of on her own, hiding the fact that both of their parents were gone, so that they could stay together. Millicent, this is my mother, Janice, and my dad, Jacob."

"We had a brief introduction with your siblings at Anthony's," Eric's mother said. "So brave of you, a child yourself, to keep your family together. It's lovely to meet you, Millicent."

"And … I'm very happy to meet you, too," Millicent said shyly. Eric's parents! She extended her hand.

"Hugs! Hugs all around," Eric's mother insisted.

"That's right," his father seconded. "Hugs all around!"

A round of hugging ensued until everyone was giggling.

Eric looked at Millicent. "Can I tell them?"

"Oh!" Millicent exclaimed. "Are you sure?"

"Of course I'm sure. Millicent has just agreed to marry me."

"*Ohhh, Sissy,*" Stephanie cried, "let me see the ring."

"Well ... I ...."

"It's right here." Eric pulled it from his pocket and put it on Millicent's finger. "We got ... interrupted before."

Millicent looked down at the ring she could barely see in the near darkness. The center stone was a simple square-cut diamond with, it appeared, smaller diamonds on either side, in a gold setting. Simple elegance. She loved it.

"Sissy, you're marrying a cowboy!" Peter cried. "That's so ... so ...."

"*Romantic*," Stephanie and Baby said together.

"I was going to say something else," Peter said. "It's so cool. A real cowboy!"

"Well, I guess he is," Millicent agreed. "Through with programming are you, cowboy?"

"I wouldn't mind. If my future wife doesn't mind."

"If I know your future wife, and I believe I do, she will want you to do what makes you happy." Millicent laughed.

Eric took her hand and kissed her ring finger.

"*Soooooo* romantic," Baby trilled.

"Hey, are you staying out there all night," Michael called from the front door.

"We're coming in," Millicent answered. "Come on in, there's so much to eat and drink," she said, even as she began to wonder who she would put where and how many beds needed to be made up.

"By the way," Eric's mother said as they wandered inside, "Clara said that she put rooms together for those of us who are a surprise to you. We'll just sneak back over there later tonight, and be back, first thing in the morning!"

"Oh!" She glanced at Eric, thinking, your mother's a mind reader.

"That's great, Mom. And, as usual, Clara is right on it. Millicent has worked tirelessly for several weeks for today. She really deserves the surprise. And a break."

"I don't need a break. But how I love the surprise!"

They all stepped inside. The air was electric with the excitement and the wonderful holiday spirit. The Spirit of Christmas Present was *present!* She was delighted to see Michael's parents again.

"Stephanie, Peter, Baby, these are Michael's parents, David and Marsha. I met them years ago, and liked them right on sight."

"And we had the same feeling about you, Millicent. We were happy he had a friend like you, as we knew he was depressed and miserable at that job. He often told us jokes that you told him. They always make us chuckle."

"Oh dear, I hope none of them were too awful."

"No, no," Michael's dad said, "Not awful at all. Cute. Sometimes just a tinge risqué. But still, cute."

"*Urg!* Embarrassment," Millicent wished she could hide her face somewhere, anywhere. "Let me continue with my introductions, and leave this subject. Michael's parents and Eric's parents are old friends, which is how I got to know Eric when he came out to be Michael's best man at the wedding. Also, being a horse whisperer, Anthony's always happy to have him give the horses attention."

"*Romantic!*" Baby said again.

Millicent laughed. "Really, she does have a vocabulary of more than one word. Don't you, Baby?"

"Yes. Of course. But if something's romantic, I'm calling it romantic."

"There's lots of food, so please, help yourselves. Plates are here. Cups are here. How old are you now Baby, I've lost track. Sixteen?"

"*Seventeen*," she replied indignantly.

"Seventeen. All right, I guess you can have some mulled wine."

"Ohh, sounds lovely."

Millicent moved into the living room and raised her voice above the convivial hubbub. "I want to thank Anthony for this wonderful surprise, bringing all our families together. It's an act of kindness and generosity that none of us will ever forget. To Anthony!"

She held her glass aloft, and everyone joined in. "To Anthony, to Anthony!"

Anthony, stood by the window, having insisted that Uncle Halian sit in the wingback chair. "Thank you, everyone. Not necessary to give me accolades. It was my present to me to see the joy this evening brings everyone. It's one thing to see the sorts of things one can do in the business world. And a very different thing to see what one can for people. For love. For one another.

"In a similar vein, I'd like the announce that Alison and I are going to get married—again. No date set, as she just said 'yes' tonight, but, of course, you're all invited!"

"*Soooooo romantic,*" Baby could be heard saying from the kitchen.

"Indeed," Anthony agreed. "*Soooooo romantic.*"

Baby stepped into the living room. "And Eric and Millicent just got engaged."

"*Really?*" Everyone exclaimed.

"Is that true?" Eaton asked.

"It is," Eric said happily.

"Perfect!" Clara nodded.

"Hey!" Tina practically bellowed. "It's supposed to be *my* night. John proposed to me, right here, out loud in front of all of you. I don't know about these other people all saying they're getting proposed to and married."

"You're right, Tina," Millicent said, "it's your night. To Tina and John!"

"To Tina and John," everyone cheered.

"Thank you," John said, coming over to Tina and putting his arm around her. "But I don't mind sharing our wonderful night with our friends. It will always be so very memorable. The Christmas Eve when there were three yeses to three proposals."

"All right, all right!" Tina pretended to grumble. "Why are you always right?"

"Not always, sweetie. But often enough to seem like it!" He laughed.

Now, Millicent thought, now would be the perfect time to turn the snow machine on. As subtly as possible she moved to the mantle and retrieved the snow machine remote control. She felt Aunt

Pelipa in the wingback chair by her watching her, but she ignored her. She pushed the button for "gentle snow." Nothing happened. She pushed the button again. Waited. Still nothing. Eric came over to stand by her.

"You're frowning. What's going on?"

"The darn snow machine won't work. Oh, that's all I wanted, was to have a bit of snow during this amazing, miraculous, evening."

"It's dear of you to want to make that beautiful picture for those you love, but, look around you. You've already done it. Not a single person is unhappy. Even Emdee is perfectly content, curled up there in the corner of the sofa with Sage."

"*Oh, Look!*" Sunitha cried out suddenly. "*Snow!*"

Millicent turned to look out the window.

"*Finally!*" She whispered to Eric. She watched the beautiful snow falling at the two windows. But then it started to come down hard.

"Oh no, it's snowing pretty heavily," she said softly to Eric. "I put it on 'gentle snow' … but at this rate, it'll soon be used up."

Baby, Lolotea, and Lonan had moved to the den to play a board game. "*Ohhhh! Snow,*" she heard Baby squeal.

The three of them burst out of the den. "*Snow!*" they exclaimed in glee. They ran outside the front door.

"*What?*" Millicent, confused, exchanged a glance with Eric, also puzzled. She, and Eric, and everyone, followed the young people outdoors.

Snow! Real, beautiful, old-fashioned, Christmas Eve, snow. The young people danced about like little children, Emdee barked and pirouetted, leaping and biting at the snow as it came down.

Clara and Eaton stood to one side, like sentries to the kingdom of snow.

Millicent felt her heart might burst with joy as she looked at everyone, the young people dancing, her little dog prancing, and each of the couples—Sage and Michael, Alison and Anthony, Tina and John, Jacob and Janice, David and Marsha—standing close together, sharing their love in the miraculous snow coming down upon them.

She looked around for Uncle Halian and Aunt Pelipa. She finally saw them in the shadows. Aunt Pelipa wore a beatific, calm smile, and Millicent knew that she had called upon the energies that swirled about the entire created universe to, this one night, bring the spirit of Christmas to their little group in the form of snow.

She put her arm around Eric, safe and happy and relaxed in the warmth of his embrace. Tomorrow was Christmas Day. Tomorrow they'd open the numerous presents, and be delighted with the things the packages revealed.

But tonight was about the gift of the miraculous snow. A present that would give them memories of love their whole, entire lifetimes. A gift that no one would ever outgrow, or become tired of, or break, or lose.

The gift of the miracle of love, the meaning of Christmas.

The tableau before her appeared as if it was a lovely, mystical snow globe, the benevolent snow a blanket of love, falling upon everyone, equally.

She smiled at Aunt Pelipa, who smiled back. They shared their secret about snow-making.

It was about ... *Love*.

The End

Dear Reader ....

I'm delighted that you've read the sweet Christmas story, *Three Proposals,* the fourth book in the *Canyon Road Love Stories* series. *Book One* is *Canyon Road, Book Two* is *One Love,* and *Book Three* is *Two Weddings.*

Sage's parents led a fascinating life in the Zuni Nation in the U.S. Southwest. Her mother wrote a beautiful paper about her people. If you'd like a free copy, write to me requesting *Life in the Pueblo*:

<u>Thea@EmersonandTilman.com</u>

About the Author

I'm a full-time writer, creating the worlds in my novels, in the Portland, Oregon area. Having lived in a variety of locations around the world, I happily settled in the beautiful Northwest, where the environment and culture are perfect for a writing life. The rain, the forests, the water falls, mountains, and ocean—plus lots of writers—make it a great place to be a writer.

Thank you beforehand for any kind review you may write—which is warmly received and much appreciated! Reviews are the life-blood of an author's career, but more importantly, I would really love to know how my book touched you.

If you have questions or comments, or would like to know about new releases of my books, write to me at the following email address. I'd love to hear from you ….

Thea@emersonandtilman.com

Thea@EmersonandTilman.com

www.ingramcontent.com/pod-product-compliance
Lightning Source LLC
Chambersburg PA
CBHW052149110526
44591CB00012B/1906